Praise for *To Be a Runner*

"Great summer beach read for the thinking runner . . . engross-
ing . . . if you're looking for the ideal running-related summer read,
look no further than *To Be a Runner*. It is characterized by a rare
combination of lightness and substance that makes it a pleasure to
read."

—Matt Fitzgerald, Competitor.com

"Anyone who has run has a story to tell as a result, and usually
behind that story is an important life lesson if we have open eyes to
see it. *To Be a Runner* shares lessons that have been learned through
the rocky, hard, sweat-filled miles as well as those miles that float
by effortlessly, with extreme joy and elation. Running is the ultimate school master. I learn something about myself, others, and life
every time I lace up my shoes and head out the door. Whether you
are a seasoned runner who can relate to the lessons shared in *To Be
a Runner* or are a beginner looking to avoid some of those painful
lessons learned by those who have gone before, you will be sure to
find some gold nuggets to take with you for your next run."

—Ryan Hall, Olympian and American record holder in the
half-marathon and cofounder of the Steps Foundation,
a growing community of radical runners stepping together
to end global poverty

TO BE A
RUNNER

HOW RACING UP MOUNTAINS, RUNNING WITH THE
BULLS, OR JUST TAKING ON A 5-K MAKES YOU A
BETTER PERSON (AND THE WORLD A BETTER PLACE)

MARTIN DUGARD

RODALE.
NEW YORK

RODALE and the Plant colophon are registered
trademarks of Penguin Random House LLC.

Originally published in hardcover and in slightly different form in
the United States by Rodale, an imprint of the Crown
Publishing Group, a division of Penguin Random House LLC,
New York, in 2011.

Library of Congress Cataloging-in-Publication Data
is available upon request.

ISBN 978-1-63565-363-2
Ebook ISBN 978-1-60961-395-2

Printed in the United States of America

Book and cover design: Christopher Rhoads
Cover photograph: Stephen Toner/Stone/Getty Images

1 3 5 7 9 10 8 6 4 2

First Paperback Edition

For Calene

CONTENTS

PAY IT FORWARD

HARD-EARNED WISDOM

AUTHOR'S NOTE

I've been asked to write this prologue and a few new essays for the paperback edition of *To Be a Runner* you now hold in your hands. I'm flattered to be asked. *TBAR* sold well in its initial release, but didn't enjoy the robust sales of the traditional how-to running books. I'd been aiming for a modern version of George Sheehan's *Running and Being,* but was blue to learn that such a market didn't seem to exist. We are a nation of runners, with more men and women participating in this sport than any other. But there is a deep division between the age-group runner whose goal is to start—and hopefully finish—a 5-K or half-marathon, and the elite racers who live for speed and suffering. My book straddled both worlds, which meant neither side really embraced it as their own. Some reviewers thought it elitist, others thought there weren't enough workout plans, and still others were looking for a memoir rather than a series of essays. I've tried to fix that last narrative thread in this edition, giving the story more of an arc. But it's still best described as adventures and misadventures from the running life, and life lessons learned along the way.

I would like you to know one thing: I love this book. I wrote it on a lark while in the Bahamas ghosting the bio of a lonely billionaire. I'd taken that gig out of desperation—the publishing world had crashed along with the rest of the economy in 2008 and I had a family to feed. Simple as that. Sometimes writing is art, but just as often writing is commerce.

Callous as that sounds, there comes a moment when the creative well needs to be plumbed. So in the midst of penning that autobiography, I took it upon myself to compose a second book. I felt like I was losing my way with words and needed to write something to restore my passion. So I chose the greatest constant in my life: running. Every day, as a simple creative exercise, I sat down and wrote an essay about the sport I have loved since I was a boy. I wrote each essay without pausing to self-edit or scrutinize the words too closely. At the end of a month, I had thirty essays. Each was about five hundred words long.

The next month was spent going over each piece, line by line. I tossed out the trite and the mean-spirited, electing for a more uplifting feel. I polished and polished some more, until the clunky stuff fell away and all I felt was flow. Then I printed out the completed manuscript, placed it in a box, tied the package in a red ribbon, and FedExed that lovely, needy chunk of my soul across the country to my agent. He is perhaps the best in the business, but Eric Simonoff is also a non-runner with whom I had a long-standing agreement that I would never, under any circumstances, write a running book.

He liked it enough to sell it. The original title was *How to Be a*

Runner, not so much as a how-to, but as a metaphorical pathway across the emotional divide between the days we choose to step out the door and push our limits and the mornings we pull the covers over our heads.

To Be a Runner was more whimsical—and a bit less pretentious. That's what stuck.

As for this new edition, part of me has been writing running essays ever since the original publication date eight years ago. I compose entire paragraphs in my head when I'm out on a trail, far away from my laptop or yellow legal pads.

I write about the people who proudly wear their heavy Disney finisher medals the last mile of a half-marathon—then drink brunch afterward. I write about the guy who dresses up as Princess Leia at the *Star Wars* races. I write about the high school cross-country team I've coached for fourteen years, and mornings like today, where my runners pushed through 1000-meter repeats in the pitch dark of a 5:30 a.m. practice, then headed straight to the weight room for thirty minutes of squats and lunges before school.

I write about my wife's friendship with her running girlfriends, and the joy it brings to her face as they hit the trail together. Sometimes, I even write about me, and my struggles to stretch, meditate, and run a few miles on those days when I'd much rather sit at my desk and write, because no form of sweat is quite so excellent as the dopamine-fueled perspiration that flows during a good run.

If you haven't read *To Be a Runner*, and perhaps know me for the history projects with my famous coauthor, I'm glad you're checking it out. Even if you're not a runner, there may be a line or word that hits you in the sweet spot of your gut. May they fortify you.

If you have read *TBAR*, thank you. I hope you enjoy revisiting the original text, and find a laugh or inspiration in these additional new essays.

If there's one thing I've learned from writing this book, it's that my own goal is to be a runner the rest of my life, a solitary figure trotting through the local canyon at whichever pace feels best on a given day.

And that is more than enough.

Martin Dugard
Rancho Santa Margarita, California
April 2019

FIRST STEPS

"Now bid me run, and I will strive with things impossible."

— SHAKESPEARE, *JULIUS CAESAR*

FIRST STEPS

All runners announce their entry into the sport with the most basic athletic action: a step. A simple foot plant that leads to thousands upon millions more: some faster, some slower; at home and around the world; in sun, blizzard, and driving rain; on pavement, dirt, mud, gravel, sand, loam, grass, oval all-weather tracks with eight lanes that measure exactly 400 meters around, and freshly scrubbed Pamplona cobblestones. A splendid step, a quiet step, a lonely step; born of some inner dialogue, some longing to be different, to be—not the best—but at least better. The step takes less than a second. Doubts are silenced in that whisper of time. Lives are changed.

Almost every modern runner, even now, can trace his or her first step to 1967, when a Dallas physician named Dr. Kenneth H. Cooper published *Aerobics*. And so can I. *Aerobics* was running's version of Mao's little red book, a revolutionary tome that spawned a movement and made us all see the world in a different way. It was as if the sun came up navy blue instead of orange one morning, then stayed that way evermore.

Aerobics has become synonymous with nylon/Lycra and synchronized group exercise set to pulsating synthesized music. There are substrata of aerobics, like high impact and low impact and body pump and even Spinning, which is basically aerobics on a stationary bike. Thanks to aerobics, there was such a garment as the Performance Thong, sold by Nike, which may or may not have been effective workout apparel but whose name offers one of the more inspired word pairings in the English language.

But back in 1967, *aerobics* (the term refers to oxygen consumption) meant just one thing: running. Dr. Cooper believed that a workout stressing the heart and lungs was an effective means of staying fit and a way to prevent keeling over at forty from a massive clogging of the arteries. With this simple premise packaged into his bestselling book, running ceased to be the sole domain of Olympians, fitness zealots, and men like Mercury astronaut John Glenn, who was considered eccentric for running three miles each day.

As all this was happening, my dad was a bomber pilot with a fondness for Spanish cigars and Bombay gin. He was also in danger of being pulled off flight status due to a recently collapsed lung. In desperation, he took up aerobics. We lived at Bunker Hill, an air force base in Indiana, soon to be renamed in memory of tragic Apollo astronaut Gus Grissom. The base gym was sponsoring a one-hundred-mile club in order to encourage running, with members' names posted on a laminated board near the towel window. For each mile run, a staff member would add a tally mark in red grease pencil next to that member's name. A hundred red marks and you were in the club. I can't remember whether there was a

T-shirt to commemorate the achievement or a next level for the truly ambitious, but at the time running one hundred miles was a very big deal. The club filled up quickly, which is to say that the board, from top to bottom, was lined with names and red marks accumulated horizontally to resemble a bar graph.

My folks both signed up. They would run two to three miles at a time, ten laps for a mile around the gym's laminated wooden basketball floor. My little brother Matt and I would play beneath the fold-out bleachers as they ran, always keeping one eye out for fallen change. Sometimes we snuck over to the board and penciled in outlaw red marks next to our mom's name. We had noticed that another woman was running several more miles per week than she was. It didn't seem right that someone else's mom would get to a hundred first.

One day, having already penciled in an auspicious amount of mileage on our mother's behalf, Matt and I came out from the shadow of the bleachers and spontaneously began running. My first step came on planks of polished hardwood, with my little brother at my side. Our goal was a mile. It seemed an impossible distance. When I think of how far a one-hundred-mile trail run feels to me today, it is very much like how a mile felt back in 1967.

I was a small, awkward child with skinny hips, a goofy smile that accentuated vampirelike canine teeth, and blond hair combed straight forward in bangs that ended an inch above my eyebrows. I looked like the very young, very towheaded love child of George Harrison and Moe, the Stooge.

Matt was even smaller, with fiery red hair and huge blue eyes. We probably looked even younger than six and five as we ran those first tentative steps in our jeans and BX sneakers. The warm gym smelled of sweat, floor wax, and leather basketballs. The distant thwack of handball games in the nearby courts drowned out our labored breathing.

Matt would go on to become a record-breaking collegiate runner. But on that day so long ago, he started walking after a few laps and then sat down. I pressed on. We had gone out too fast. I had to drastically slow my pace to keep going. After five laps I was about to quit, but the young airman working the towel counter bellowed encouragement as I chugged past. For the first time in my life, I felt the galvanizing burst of adrenaline that comes from being cheered on. I kept going.

After seven laps I was close to stepping off the track, when my parents lapped me and added their own words of praise. There was surprise in their voices and a relieved sort of pride, as if they'd been secretly worried that the athlete gene had skipped a generation. After eight laps I was fairly certain I would finish but thought I might have to walk the rest. But that would mean I had not technically run a mile, so I banished all thoughts of walking.

After nine laps, my legs were so heavy that the final circuit loomed like a mile unto itself. There was no thought about proper form or looking good. I just prayed that I would finish. Hail Marys. Our Fathers. Nonstop lobs to heaven, pleading that God would carry me. I was a year from making my First Communion. Spontaneous prayer was as automatic as giving up chocolate for Lent.

With thirty yards left, I kicked it in.

There was no cheering crowd at the finish line—only Matt, who wasn't all that impressed. But to hear my folks talk as we stepped out into the humid Indiana summer and squeezed into our wood-paneled Ford Country Squire, you would have thought I'd just made the Olympic team. When I watched Jim Ryun racing Kip Keino in Mexico City on television the next year, I hatched a lifelong dream of doing just that.

On the day I ran my first mile, I didn't understand the concept of something "coming naturally." But I learned that distance running wasn't so tough for me. In fact, I liked it very much. I've considered myself a runner ever since.

Running has taken me on adventures great and small, at home and around the world. It has provided me with hope and perseverance on days when I had none—and even, once every great while, warmed me with that fleeting ray of sunshine known as glory. Running has taught me that I can do anything, just so long as I keep putting one foot in front of the other. Sometimes that notion is metaphorical and sometimes not. In this way, I have been inspired to attempt things I would have never dreamed possible.

And it all started with a single step.

BASE MILES

The primal tug to run whispers in our ears. It calls to us even when we pretend that running is just for athletes or children or the very thin. In that way, being a lapsed runner is like being a lapsed Catholic: Whether out the front door of your house or into the front door of the church, you're always just one step away from being right back in.

The first time I got fat was when I quit running after more than a decade of competition, then continued to stuff calories down my throat like a man training a hundred miles a week. No food group was safe. I completely cast aside the disciplines of being a racer. Giving up running and morphing into a larger—though, unfortunately, not jollier—version of myself was an act of defiance that quickly led me into a personal wilderness. It was running that eventually led me back out. The in-between was not easy, but it was the making of me and set me on the path I have followed ever since.

That, however, is another saga for another day. For now let's just say that I was trying to live the Hunter S. Thompson lifestyle without the Hunter S. Thompson constitution.

My four-year hiatus from running got so bad that when I told people I'd raced at the collegiate level, their response was to arch their eyebrows as if they'd caught me in a rather obvious lie. My lowest point came when a friend asked if I was capable of running three miles. He was new to running and had that shiny, happy look of all new converts. I found him incredibly annoying.

"Of course," I joked, knowing it was not true but remembering the days when I could pop off an easy ten-miler before breakfast, then back it up with five more in the afternoon.

This day, however, a mile was too much. Three was a sheer impossibility.

The second time I got fat was because my brother and sister died too young. I poured my grief into work. Once again, I gave up the sport that had sustained my emotional and physical health for so many years. That particular era ended with me running with the bulls in Pamplona, bursting with a new appreciation for life and my God-given talent for running—a talent you appreciate very much when a bull singles you out of a crowd and chases you up and over the six-foot-high red wall of a bull-fighting arena.

But that is also another story for another day—perhaps later in this book.

My point is not weight gain or weight loss. It's what those two periods have in common: new beginnings. The only way I could regain my fitness and active lifestyle was to pretend I'd never run a mile in my life, then start the long journey back by taking that first step out the door.

In physiological terms it's known as base miles. In his book *Daniels' Running Formula*, Dr. Jack Daniels points out that "participants in any sport need to spend time subjecting the body to low-intensity stress, mainly to prepare the body for high-intensity training." The point is to reacquaint the body with sustained movement. Ligaments and tendons get sturdier. The body builds more red blood cells and becomes more efficient at transporting oxygen. Capillary networks become more elaborate, and the body as a whole becomes more fine-tuned and efficient.

You run base miles at a conversational pace—that is, you should be able to have an easy conversation while running them. This might seem to imply that base miles are easy. And in time, they are. But that first step out the door, and the thousands of steps that follow during each and every one of those come-to-Jesus training sessions that make up a comeback, are anything but easy. They are a reminder of how far I've fallen and how far I've got to go. I wonder if I will ever know real speed again.

The process is deliberately slow. Every June, when my teams begin base miles for cross-country season, veteran runners are amazed that a five-miler seems painful. New runners are astounded when I ask them to run more than a mile without stopping. This is the time when we focus on stretching, weight lifting, movement exercises, and strengthening the tibialis anterior muscle to prevent the dreaded shin splints, which can become chronic if not dealt with proactively.

A few weeks after that first workout, I won't be able to keep up with the top runners, but during the early base phase I run alongside them. It's a time of storytelling and dreams, when they share their hopes for the season and on into college, and I reassure them that they'll get there. See, running base miles isn't just about strengthening the body. It's also a time to whip the mind into shape with nurturing and affection. Gentle doses of discipline such as hill repeats and tempo runs remind the most powerful of all muscles that it needs to be ten times tougher than any ligament or tendon.

That's the way it was with me back in my midtwenties, as I contemplated a return to running. I'd sworn it off as a vestige of childhood. Running was my dad's domain, and to leave the sport behind was to assert my independence from him. Over time, however, what I missed about the sport wasn't the stuff that induces running nirvana: I didn't miss the endorphin rushes or morning runs or even the close bond that comes with training alongside committed teammates. No, what I missed was ambling out the door and finding a new trail, then following wherever it might lead. I'd drive along the freeway and see hills or wilderness that I'd once roamed, now unattainable because I'd let myself go in the name of free will or independence or finding myself—whatever you want to call it.

One day, I just had enough. I slipped on an old pair of shoes, found a pair of shorts that fit, and then chuffed out for a run. My body still knew what it was supposed to do. So though I was almost twice my former competitive running weight (I would like to pretend that I am exaggerating, but it feels strangely cathartic to admit the truth), muscle memory made me run tall, not hunched over. My hips were forward, my shoulders were back, and my legs tried their best to lope. They failed. I trudged a half-mile without stopping.

The next day I did it again. Then I took a week off, because it all seemed like a waste of time. I'd just have to accept the fact that running really belonged to my dad and not me. I was a big guy now, and I'd have to find some sort of big guy pursuit to match my level of fitness. I can't quite remember what that was supposed to be—rugby, I guess. Sumo. Something where people collide.

Then I saw an advertisement for a triathlon. It was just ten weeks away. I hadn't swum laps in forever, I didn't own a bike, and running was in my past. But something about that challenge seemed like a way to return to running on my own terms. Before I could convince myself otherwise, I paid the entry fee and changed my life. I started getting up early again. I found a pool and bashed through lap after lap. I borrowed a bike and bought cool bike clothes and shoes.

And I forced myself to run.

Mile after miserable, painful, wretched mile, I forced myself to forget the runner I'd once been and just tried to get myself fit enough to run the 6.2 miles required of the triathlon.

Not all the weight came off by race day, but a lot did. I was looking and feeling something like my old self. It was my twenty-fifth birthday, and suddenly I had a sense of hope and purpose to my life again. I felt in charge. I felt independence. I felt all those things I'd spent the previous four years trying in vain to feel.

Strange how the way out of the wilderness is very often the same as the way in.

Later that night, I celebrated with friends by attending a Lone Justice concert, then asking a special girl out for a first date. I'd been flirting with her for a few weeks but hadn't had the confidence to do much about it. She accepted. Two years later, we married. More than thirty years later, she's still my special girl.

It was base miles and the strength to compete in that triathlon that gave me the confidence to ask Calene for that date. I'd almost quit during the swim because someone kicked off my goggles in the first 200 yards, even as some other competitor swam right over me. The lake water was cold and murky green. I began to hyperventilate and decided right then that triathlons weren't for me. That was when I learned a curious thing about open-water swimming—to quit, one must actually travel back to shore. Vested in that logic, it made just as much sense to keep swimming.

I did better on the bike. But by the time I got into the second transition area and prepared to run my first race in four years, my legs had had enough. I tried to tell them how far they'd come in just a few short weeks, but they weren't having any of it. So I talked to myself instead, reminding myself that I had once been a runner and possessed the mental strength to see myself through this challenge. My legs would just have to come along for the ride.

The first mile was uphill—Alicia Parkway, right on Olympiad, all the way to the sky. I drive that road every day now. Doesn't seem that far in a car. But on that June morning it loomed like the Great Wall, a mental and physical barrier that seemed as if it would climb upward forever and ever. Cresting the summit felt like a pipe dream.

Then, at the base of the hill, just outside that transition area, there stood my dad. He was dressed to run. I didn't know he was going to be there. He'd just showed up.

The last time we had run together was ten years earlier. Since then, we'd even gotten out of the habit of talking.

He fell in beside me.

"How you doing?" he asked.

"Not so good."

"You can do this."

When I think of my favorite moments with my dad, it's times like those, when I misjudged how much I needed him or how much he wanted to see me be my best. More than anything, when someone you love believes in you, you feel like you can do anything.

I wouldn't have had that moment without the wilderness that came before it and the base miles that followed. My friend Gerard Fusil likes to say that sometimes you have to go through hell to get to heaven. I believe that. I also believe he stole that saying from a Steve Miller song, but it sounds more profound when a Frenchman says it.

So as my runners grouse about the aches and pains of their base miles and wonder if they will ever know the effortless speed that comes with peak performance, I gently tell them to persevere and show up for practice every day, ready to log those early runs.

Because base miles, whatever wilderness you're wandering through, will give you the strength and confidence to find a way out.

RUN DATES

When I first met my wife and was so mesmerized by her hotness that I needed to do something extraordinary to convince her I was the real deal, I got in the habit of attending her 6 a.m. aerobics class. This was back when closing time was an early night for me. To my way of thinking, bouncing around in a room full of strangers at the crack of dawn was a sure demonstration that Cupid's arrow had struck. Every morning when I jumped out of bed instead of hitting the snooze button, it was with the quiet prayer that she felt the same way.

Calene was the instructor. She'd stand up at the front and lead group exercise, cueing the music just so and generally acting as head cheerleader. There would be coeds, businesswomen, housewives, a few guys who'd ventured out of the weight room, and lovestruck me.

I'd stand in the back, trying desperately to find the beat and follow the choreography. Now and then Calene would smile my way, which always made my heart soar. She was a vision in her leotard, eighties headband, and leg warmers, bopping around to Def Leppard

and Madonna. I was madly in love. Aerobics wasn't my thing—far
from it. I was much more comfortable running the trails just
outside the gym. But I was dating the instructor, which was
awesome. And every day, through practice and perseverance, I was
getting the hang of aerobics.

Or so I thought. After a few weeks of 6 a.m.'s, Callie and I
made an aerobics date of sorts. A friend of hers was teaching a class
on Saturday. We stood together in the back. The music was new.
The footwork was new. The room was packed. It seemed like whenever the rest of the aerobicizers were going right, I would be going
left, bumping into complete strangers, my sweatiness and lack of
coordination all too obvious. But it was okay, I thought. I was in the
back. I was invisible. I watched the clock as the hour ticked down,
more and more sure with each passing sweep of the red second
hand that I would survive.

It was not to be. The instructor had noticed. How could she
not? I was bouncing off people, raising my hands when I should
have been extending them to the side, and spinning in circles when
I should have been stepping straight back and forth. I would not
have been more obvious if I'd wrapped myself in a red cape and
yelled "Toro!"

The instructor strolled down the center of the floor, all those
swaying bodies parting like the Red Sea. She had a pretty smile. I
was flustered at first by her attention, in an embarrassment-of-
riches way. How could this be? How could this be that a mere
mortal male such as myself was somehow desired by not one but
two beautiful aerobics instructors? Was it my bed-head hair? My

runner's biceps? Or maybe it was the socks that were going on their third use without a wash? And now these Aphrodites exercised, one on either side of me, their movements synched to the music, lavishing me with their loveliness and physicality.

In that instant I let myself believe there was finally something special about me. I let myself believe that after years of struggle and self-doubt, I radiated poise and savoir faire. I felt like D'Artagnan, who, for my money, is the most dashing of the musketeers.

Clearly, this certain special something was now obvious to the universe—and, by extension, to a most special breed of woman blessed with keen wit, athleticism, and extraordinary beauty.

I smiled. They smiled back.

The instructor wore a cordless mic. The volume was extremely loud. She prodded me in vain to fall in lockstep with her movements. The entire class quickly became aware that I was rhythmically inept. I began perspiring more and more, like a flop-sweat sprinkler system. Flecks of water tossed from my hair and the tips of my fingers, the sweat and spasticity giving me a Mansonesque dementia.

"You can do it," the instructor chided.

That's right. Chided. As if to a child. Like to the five-year-old who colors outside the lines.

I tried harder.

"Okay. Try again," she insisted. Her tone was irksome, telling the whole class that she was doing her damnedest, but there was absolutely no helping the guy in the back who was now in grave danger of permanently losing the affection of at least one aerobics admirer.

It was useless. We all knew it.

"Well," the instructor informed one and all as she bounced back up to her podium, "I guess you just march to the beat of a different drummer."

That moment felt like equal parts shame and embarrassment. But it was a necessary turning point. After that class, I never set foot on an aerobics floor again. Even after Calene and I got married and had kids, there was a deep divide in our workout patterns. She was the gym girl, the one who taught step and Spin and all those other group exercise classes ("Group X," in gym parlance). Her training followed a tidy pattern of classes, weights, stretching, a shower, and then grabbing our sons from the gym's childcare before pushing the stroller over to Starbucks. Me, I was still the sweaty mess, earning my endorphins on the ridges and forests above our town. Once I shed that pesky swimming component of triathlon, there wasn't a single organized or structured aspect to my training. Whether on the mountain bike or a run, I just kind of made it up as I went along, marching to that different drummer pounding out his little off-kilter beat in my prefrontal cortex.

I don't remember a single incident that caused the change. Maybe it was buying Callie that Specialized mountain bike for Christmas. Maybe it came when she got tired of planning her day around Group X class schedules. Or maybe it was just one of those things. She had always been a runner, but Callie started logging more miles outdoors than on a treadmill. Soon she was asking if I'd show her a few trails, so that she and her girlfriends might know the way.

Those first marital trail runs were not an easy time. My mistakes were twofold. First, I misjudged mileage, thinking that two miles were one and four miles were two or three. This, in turn, led to a new level of exasperation on my wife's part. It's not that she thought her husband was a complete moron, though I do think the term *clueless* was bandied about on more than one occasion. And I distinctly remember her screaming "What is wrong with you?" after one overly long outing on a ninety-degree July morning. She was not, for the record, inquiring about my physical health.

This is where I learned the hard truth that when you tell someone that they are about to go out for a three-mile run, returning seventy-five minutes later and trying to pass off all those hills and singletrack as a mere three makes one look delusional. Which brings me to my second big mistake: I thought my wife would enjoy meandering as much as I do. When I leave the house or set out from a trailhead, I never have a planned course. I go left when I feel like it, or right if the trail looks appealing. Some days I go fast, some days very slow. It all depends where my head is. My only parameter is time. As long as I make it back within my allotment, the run is ideal.

Not so when running with my wife. A route is a route is a route. Adding to or deviating from is a violation of the prerun trust.

Until then, I never knew that preknowledge of a run course actually makes it mentally more doable and delays the onset of fatigue (studies have since borne this out, which is why I have my team jog any new cross-country course a couple of hours before a race). Making matters worse, my wife is not one to back down from a challenge. So when I would study a deer trail tacking side to side up an endless hillside and wonder aloud, "Hey, why don't we see where that goes?" my wife never backed down. She complained, in her own sweet way. She did not, however, back down.

I was churlish at first, reluctant to share my alone time out on the trails. But over time I came to enjoy our runs a great deal. I liked the conversation. I liked the time with my wife. And most of all, I liked that there was something we did together that seemed to exist outside of time or schedules, in a place of beauty and serenity. We ran, we talked, we connected in a way that was often impossible in a houseful of growing boys.

And so I learned to be a better running partner. I needed to temper that inner drummer and find a middle ground between his beat and Calene's. Everyone likes to finish a run feeling successful. Somehow, that wasn't happening. If anything, Callie was growing more and more frustrated. She was like me back in that aerobics class, with a running partner every bit as cloying as that chiding instructor.

So now I have two kinds of runs. There are Marty runs, where I go out and play with speed and course and time. And there are run dates, the kind that usually take place each Thursday morning after the boys get off to school. We trot a local trail for about an hour, we catch up, and then we go have coffee. It is a cheap date, to be sure. But it is my favorite kind.

The loneliness of the long-distance runner is overrated. Like all the best things in life, a great run becomes even more wondrous when shared with someone you love.

SMOOTH

The trail I run more than any other is muddy right now. The stream below the bridge is up. Winter rains have beaten down the dry grass lining the path. It is an out-and-back course that offers the prospect of a greater loop if I feel like going long. The first two miles lead away from the ocean ten miles west, up to the top of Saddleback Mountain. A gate into a public park marks the end of that portion of the run. Most days, this is the turnaround.

To the casual observer, there is no uphill grade on the outbound. But a runner can feel it. You can sense the way you lean ever so slightly into the earth and the way you labor just a little bit more than you would expect. The oak trees forming a canopy near the mile mark, where I saw a bobcat the other day, don't whiz past the way they would at speed. On some days, when I'm stiff or just out for some shake-and-bake morning miles to clear my head before writing, those two miles are a grind. There is no nice way to say it.

The return is something else entirely. The great Czech runner Emil Zatopek liked to say that "the border between Pain and Suffering is what separates the men from the boys." But there is a level just south of Pain, and long before Suffering, that feels like floating. This is the training zone that coaches like to call tempo.

I call it that, too. But when I am in it, feeling it, grooving on it, reveling in it, *tempo* seems too benign a term. The sensation ricocheting around my body is something I like to call Smooth.

That ever-so-incidental uphill of the outbound two miles becomes a nice little shove from behind once the slope works in my favor. On really long, hot runs I might challenge myself to tempo that section, if only to get home to the fifty/fifty mixture of ice water and Coca-Cola that is my favorite postrun fluid replacement beverage. But even on a morning wake-up trot, the downhill grade calls to me, asking that I open up the stride and hasten my rhythm. Smooth feels good. Smooth feels easy. Smooth feels, to give it a corporate context, like synergy.

Sometimes things get to clicking too well. I push the pace harder. There's more urgency to my breathing and less suppleness to my gait. And then Smooth is gone. I've gone from tempo to racing. Some days I keep pushing until I have crossed that border between Pain and Suffering. And that's okay if that's what I'm in the mood for. A good personal ass-kicking never did anyone harm.

But most days I dial it back to Smooth. I've learned that if my body is reassured that a run will be conducted at this optimal pace and I won't trick it into going any faster, the motivation to get out the door for the run comes easier. So unless I am feeling particularly blindingly, effortlessly fast, I keep that promise.

Some days I find a loophole during a long run and settle into

Smooth with five or six miles to go. My body cooperates, but only so long as I don't continue the charade and push into Zatopek country.

Tempo hovers just below the body's lactate threshold level, where it is theorized that the most efficient training takes place. The sustained effort forces the body to find balance and efficiency at a speed much faster than a walk or a slow plod. I remember once running with four or five really fit guys down the canyon road into Laguna Beach. We kept a hard tempo going for almost an hour. About thirty minutes in, the euphoria of an endorphin rush washed over me, and I knew exactly how it felt to run effortlessly at speed. It wasn't a heart-rate thing that could be tracked by a band around my chest, or anything having to do with a stopwatch. It was the sun and the moon and the stars and the pavement and my legs and my shoes and my lungs and my brain and the running buddies who had found this awesome pace, converging into aerobic threshold ambrosia.

Who wouldn't want to learn that?

Striving to understand tempo not only teaches someone to run better and longer, but it's such a function of feel and body awareness that it's invaluable in teaching someone how to race properly. A couple of ticks slower and they're lapsing into long slow distance. One tick faster and they're taxing heart and lung systems that can't sustain the effort as long.

Runners need to know that tempo running is not the same as race pace, unless the race is at least ten miles.

I have this theory that the life well lived takes place in the tempo zone: pushing limits but not burning the candle at both ends, knowing where you stop and other people begin, and generally striving to find that sweet spot where each and every moment is Smooth.

Right now I feel this way. I went to bed last night thinking about what I was going to write this morning. I woke up eager and aching to sit down and put those thoughts on paper. If I can write every day, run every day, minimize the clutter on my desk, and treat the people around me with love and courtesy (and that means when I get cut off on the freeway, too, which takes some doing), then my attitude and outlook will be just that much more fantastic. If I don't do those things, there is a very good possibility I will lapse into decay or lethargy or simply feel overwhelmed to the point of sputtering inertia.

An example is the time my oldest son called from college to talk about the stress of finals week. He commented that his room was a mess and he hadn't worked out in forever. My wife, who has seen the anxieties of the father passed on to the son, insisted that he clean his room and go for a run. Suffice it to say that the young man who texted back a couple of hours later was calmer.

Last year, I decided to undertake the great adventure of turning something I'd written into a movie. There was nothing Smooth about the process. I found little time to run, each answered phone call brought some new absurd demand or problem, and financing was so tight that even the joy of being on set and seeing the words I'd written emoted by famous professional actors was overshadowed by the task of finding money to shoot another day. I would drive home around midnight and crawl exhausted into bed. My mind never shut down. So it should have been no surprise that on two occasions I went sleepwalking. One time my wife found me in the backyard. The other time I was in the shower at 3 a.m., insisting that I was needed on the set. My wife began hiding my car keys before bed.

Now, I'm not saying that a life at tempo pace is a life without problems. By its very nature, tempo is a demanding level of running. Life should be no different. The trick is having the mental and physical self-awareness to keep pushing limits to find that supple zone, knowing that you're getting stronger and faster and better with each new challenge. Producing that movie was not a Smooth experience, but there's no way I would have been able to handle that challenge without the strength I had gained from running in that sweet spot.

Smooth is difficult. We're barraged each day by information, always in contact with other human beings, thanks to phone and e-mail and text. Even when we turn the radio off in the car to groove on a moment of silence, the mental burden of driving in heavy traffic is hardly conducive to introspection. There are days I head out on my trail and mistake a purposeful trot for Smooth. There are also some days I mistake the sudden impulse to run hill repeats for Smooth, too. But I keep looking for that ambrosia, content in the knowledge that if I center myself and listen to the still, small voice inside my head, the rest of life will be very Smooth indeed.

FORE!

I can't remember when I fell in love with running on golf courses. It's like trying to remember the sweetness of a first kiss or on which warm French summer morning the gooey pungency of Normandy Camembert rocked my world. An easy run on the velvety tundra of a golf course energizes the mind and body. The footing is easy. There's no sensation of pounding, because you feel only downy softness and hear the soft rustle of grass. The earth swoops, soars, and buckles. Bunkers and rough and fairway and bending contours are playful obstacles. All around, the landscape as far as the eye can see is a vibrant shade of green. It's as if you've popped out for a run and been transported to Ireland.

Some researchers believe in a condition known as biophilia. This is defined as an innate longing to be one with nature. Biophilia is why sitting on a park bench can make one feel so content. Or why we long to escape when stuck indoors on a glorious afternoon.

Golf is a societally approved method of overdosing on biophilia. Yet it has crossed my mind more than once that golf courses are wasted on golfers, with their plodding pace, electric carts, and so-serious demand for hush and focus. To run a golf course is the exact opposite—the pace becomes a carefree bound, there's certainly no need for a cart, and the mind disdains the serious as each step makes the run feel less and less like a workout and more like a child's idea of playtime.

When I think of My Favorite Runs Ever, golf courses always make the list. I think of the links at Turtle Bay Resort on Oahu at the crack of dawn, with its vestigial World War II pillboxes and balmy Pacific breezes. And that sloping course with the broad fairways next to the Westin on Maui. I think of Kota Kinabalu, on the island of Borneo, where the links segue from manicured greenery to cobra-infested jungle in a matter of inches. I think of the course at Mather Air Force Base, the course here in my town, and a dozen other places around the world over which I've rambled. I revel not only in their beauty but also in the inadvertent courtesy: Golf courses are nothing if not convenient. They are arranged in linear fashion, so that an eighteen-hole adventure is as simple as playing connect-the-dots from green to green; there's always free parking (though in the name of trespassing, it's sometimes better to park off-site); and, no matter where I go, course designers have been kind enough to place restrooms and cold water fountains at random intervals along the path, just in case I need a break.

How thoughtful.

As a golfer myself, I know what it means to be a considerate course user. So that I don't interfere with the players, my runs take place just before dawn, as ground crews trim the fairways by their mowers' headlights. They wave at me. I wave back. We have the bond that comes from leaving a warm bed too early. They see that I'm careful and considerate, treating my beloved golf course run as a privilege born out of that 5 a.m. wake-up.

I never run through the sand traps, thinking of the poor golfer whose ball might land in the depressions caused by my footfalls. I never run on the greens, because it's almost sacrilegious. I like to stay just off the fairway, where the rough gets heavy. The dense grass adds more cushion and makes me work harder. Five or six miles of that stuff will deaden your calves in a hurry.

Just as conscientiously, I avoid the concrete cart paths at all costs. Once, my depth perception compromised in the nonexistent predawn light, I stepped from grass onto cart path, thinking they were the same level. In fact, the cart path was a good four inches lower. When I landed, my foot was already anticipating an advanced section of the gait cycle. Which is to say that it had rolled slightly to deflect shock. It wasn't the bottom of my shoe that plunged to the concrete first—it was the bone on the outside of my ankle. I had to half crawl, half limp home. The bruise ran up my calf like a purplish-black racing stripe. I couldn't flex my foot, let alone run, for three weeks.

In the Midwest, on the East Coast, and everywhere else that actually has seasons, golf courses double as cross-country stadiums each autumn. Winter freeze and snow will restore the land, erasing the adverse effects of hundreds of racers rubbing away the grass on pivotal corners and creating patches of shoe-stealing mud where the earth is too wet.

Not so in California, where the weather's warm. The courses are twelve months of stress relief and competitive escape for golfers and a thriving business for the courses. Runners are not only unwelcome; we are pariahs. Even public courses, which I would argue should be considered truly public thanks to their tax-based funding, are appalled that runners might tread their hallowed turf.

This is when running becomes trespassing. If I'm caught, it will be by a course marshal making his early morning course sweep. I won't have seen him because I'm so lost in the run. He will pull up alongside me in his cart and say that I need to leave immediately. I am always polite. Marshals are not. Course marshals behave like vassals whose feudal lord has commanded them to smite interlopers. I'm surprised they don't ride horses and carry broadswords.

This is when I remind the marshal that this is a public course and I am a tax-paying citizen. That gives them pause. Seriously. They give me a perplexed look that says they never thought of it like that. My argument makes sense. I trot off and escape, making a mental note to keep a more watchful eye for marshals in the future.

But that doesn't always work. One time it wasn't a course marshal but a senior member of the grounds crew whom I encountered. His feudal lord's commands coursed through his veins like a power potion. He drove up beside me and tried to grip me by the scruff of my neck while commanding me to stop. I don't know about you, but when anyone tries to grab me like a nun apprehending a misbehaving second grader, stopping is the last thing on my mind.

My adrenaline kicked in. The speed that comes with anger and fear made me run faster. I was sprinting over hill and dale, a madman in a golf cart driving alongside me. I calmly (and somewhat breathlessly) reminded him that this was a public course. He denied this reality and said he was going to place me under citizen's arrest and put me in jail. Absurd as it sounded at that tranquil morning hour—surrounded on all sides by dew-covered grass and the sweet silence of dawn—he was serious. I ran faster. At top speed, the golf cart and I were traveling the exact same pace.

My pursuer then made a grave mistake. Planning to tackle me, he angled the golf cart along the right side of my body. He aimed the steering wheel straight down the fairway and then hurled his torso at mine. My last image of him was over my shoulder. He was sprawled on that fresh-cut morning grass. His cart was slowing to a halt. He was screaming about the citizen's arrest. And I was striding safely home.

I won that battle but lost the war. Worrying about grown men leaping at me from golf carts isn't my idea of easy mileage. I don't run there anymore. Well, at least not as much as I used to.

I've stopped most other forms of trespassing as well. I used to have a standard that said it was okay to hop a fence and run through a wilderness area belonging to some great corporate entity, just so long as that land was slated for development. Sadly, the reason I stopped is because all that land has been developed.

Now and again I have my moments. Just yesterday I went for a run and came across a woman on horseback. She had a regal air and a stiff back. "Hi," I said, standing to one side of the trail so her horse wouldn't spook.

She looked straight forward. It was as if the trail was her personal fairway and I had intruded.

The woman wore a sweater emblazoned with the crest of a tony country club. I know that country club. I know the development built up around it. And I know its golf course.

I used to run that land back when it was the sort of cactus-and-sycamore-covered great wide open that only trespassing runners and herds of cows found beautiful. One afternoon I came across a calf that had wandered into a thicket of cactus on a deer path and was too terrified to walk itself back out. The mother knew better. She was standing just outside the prickly thicket, mooing loudly for assistance. I didn't know much about cows, but I couldn't bear to imagine that calf stuck in there as day fell into night, easy prey for coyotes and mountain lions. I stopped my run and tiptoed into the cactus, then lifted the scared calf into my arms. To show its gratitude, its rear end deposited a stream of brown runny matter all over my arms and running shorts. Cows do that when they're terrified, as I found out.

I plopped the calf onto the ground in front of her mother and looked up to see a weathered old cowboy approaching on horseback. He was what they used to call ramrod thin, with unblinking eyes and tanned brown skin stretched over his face. He was eighty, if a day. When he died years later, his obituary said that he was the last true vaquero in Southern California. He'd been riding that land for almost fifty years. It might as well have been his own. In a way, I think it was.

I felt like the peasant in *Monty Python and the Holy Grail,* the one who knows for certain that a stranger must be the king because he doesn't have shit all over him.

"I was just trying to help," I explained.

"I was watching you." He didn't fill in the extra words that would make the situation more comfortable. This would have been nice, seeing as how I had, you know, shit all over me.

"Look, is it okay if I'm out here?" In those days, I ran those trails at least five times a week. There were other places to run but nothing as serene and perfect. Fact was, we both knew the land would soon become a subdivision.

He took his time thinking about it. "Long as you don't hurt my cows or cut my fences, I'm alright with that."

"I don't, uh, cut fences," I reassured him, holding out my hands to show I bore no wire cutters. He just nodded. With a small wave that I hoped looked stoic, I turned and headed for the other side of the fence, two miles away. I looked back a couple of hundred yards later. He was still sitting there on his horse in the exact same spot, making sure I left his cows alone.

I hadn't thought about that cowboy in forever until yesterday, when I saw that woman with her country club sweater, the one that said I was an outsider in her world. I had the quiet satisfaction of knowing that after that canyon had been developed and all the sycamores and cactus had been bulldozed and all the cows sent to graze somewhere in Alberta and the inevitable golf course was built—I still had the inspiration to trespass one fine dewy morning and run those brand-new eighteen holes—the same eighteen holes represented by the logo.

I think if some course marshal had ridden out to citizen's arrest me, I would have had to explain that my being there was perfectly legal. For though it was a private course, I hadn't bothered any cows and I hadn't cut any fences. That cowboy was as close to a feudal lord as I will ever know.

And we had a deal.

A Breather

The House of Pain is a simple gym. Actually, it's not even a gym. It's an office space in a residential business park. A mortgage broker resides next door, and a banner company just moved out across the parking lot. Twice each week I drive to that nondescript lot, wedging my Suburban between the cars of people who actually work and wear business attire at 10 a.m. I'll walk across the parking lot barefoot, shoes in hand. I usually wear a sweatshirt to help me get warm, knowing that I will either discard it after the first twenty minutes or vomit from the excess heat and exertion caused by wearing too many layers. Sometimes I choose the latter.

Once I step inside that small space, it's all work. Sedge directs me to a treadmill for a short jog, then layer by layer, body part by body part, he lowers me into the abyss. Things go from conversational to brutal in subtle fashion. There are no clocks in the House of Pain, nothing to say that there's forty minutes left or just fifteen. Time is marked in repetitions, exhaustion, and the number of times I need to remind myself to push harder. It's possible to enter the House of Pain and talk your way through the hour, doing the exercises at half speed, barely breaking a sweat. Some folks do it. There's no harm in that. But that's not why I come.

At some moment in each session, when I am least expecting it, Sedge instructs me to get water and rest. Back before I knew the value of this interlude, and my foolish pride had me thinking that I'd be less than manly to accept his offer, I'd do ridiculous things to keep going. I'd drop to the floor and do burpees, for instance, instead of just standing still and sipping that oh-so-sweet cold refreshment. Or I'd compulsively do lunges or sprint around the building. Really, it was just dumb.

One day I was too beaten down to care. I ripped off my sweat-shirt and dropped its soggy mass to the ground, then chugged a bottle of water in a single guzzle.

I need you to have a visual of Sedge. He is a former member of the Canadian national rugby team, with the build and appearance of Mr. Clean. He does not smile unless I am in great physical pain. I think this is because he knows he brought about this condition, and he feels some sense of personal fulfillment. It's the way I look when I write a good sentence, so I know how he feels. But when my hands are on my knees, my breath comes in short gasps, and the contents of my stomach are very close to launching them-selves into those bushes right outside HOP's front door (hurling inside is forbidden, even in the bathroom), I cannot appreciate this subtlety.

But on that day I noticed a difference in Sedge. Rather than being upset that I took a rest break or thinking less of me, he looked relieved. It was as if he'd been waiting for me to have that aha moment. Soon I found out why. That short break was no more than forty-five seconds long, but my body had just enough recovery to find new strength for the second half of the workout. I was able to work harder and thus see greater results. It's safe to say that at the end of the session, I had accomplished more—and gained more—than at any other time in the six-plus years I've been handing my body over to Sedge for what he openly refers to as torture.

Even on that small scale, the concept that rest could equal strength rocked my world. I am a creature of hard work. One of the greatest compliments someone can give me is to praise my work ethic. "Keep pushing . . . always" is my motto, a subtle reminder that those who take it easy get left behind. How incredibly liberating to think that rest, balanced with hard work, could actually be a source of strength.

I'm still trying to wrap my mind around that one. When I think of rest, I think of the next-door neighbor who used to flop onto his sofa every Sunday and spend the day alternating between napping, drinking beer, and watching football. I tried it one day—for about an hour. Not only did my body insist that I cease that vegetative state, but I felt guilty for sitting still. And while I managed to maintain the illusion of rest by remaining in my favorite chair, the truth is that I spent the day multitasking. If I wasn't planning in my journal, I had the computer out, checking e-mail and making notes about this project or that. It was all I could do not to get up and do something active.

So who was healthier? Physically, me. Emotionally, probably that neighbor. He had an amazing ability to recharge on the weekends, husbanding stores of mental and physical energy for the workweek to come. I just stormed through my daily routine, heedless of the need for downtime. When I do this for extremely long periods of time, it leads to what my wife calls New Orleans syndrome. The name comes from an epic road trip around the country that we took just before putting our college degrees to work by seeking gainful employment. I pushed myself so hard during that trip, not getting enough sleep and driving more miles in a day than a normal person was capable of doing. (My philosophy being that anything a normal person could do, an endurance athlete could do twice as well for twice as long.) By the time we got to New Orleans, my body shut down. While Calene toured the French Quarter, I lay catatonic in our hotel room. Drapes closed, lights off, body racked by aches and pains, delirious in my need for rest. The tragic part is that I recovered, only to repeat the cycle on the homebound leg, this time in Phoenix.

Even more tragic is that I am still unable to shut it down. A few years back, I had a bad case of the flu, yet I went for a ten-mile run in the morning and proceeded on to a scheduled appointment. As luck would have it, I was visiting the set of *The Contender*, a reality show about boxing. So when my body crashed and I began stumbling from lack of electrolytes, then fell to the ground and banged my forehead on the concrete, the attending physician was a fight doctor. I lay there in a small room right next to the boxing ring while a grown man in sneakers and a pinky ring reached into his little black bag for the Gatorade that brought me back around. It was a surreal way to be reminded that I have limits.

Problem is, I know better. "Many athletes think that training hard day after day will make them better runners, but the truth is that a day off will do them more good than another hard day of running," writes Dr. Joe Vigil in *Road to the Top*. Peter Coe suggests "relaxed amusement" to "avoid or overcome staleness." And Dr. Jack Daniels says that one planned "rest from running" month each year actually makes for better long-term performance.

Vigil calls rest the compensation phase. He notes that the body replenishes energy stores, oxygen-carrying red blood cells, and any other metabolic substrate that has been used up during the period of stimulus. He goes on to add the best part about rest: "The reaction is such that it will exceed the normal biological state, and greater stores of energy will be available during the next stimulus." In other words, rest makes us stronger. Which works both in life and in running.

So why am I bad at resting? Here's what happens when I rest: I allow all those nagging doubts and fears in my subconscious to come out and play. All the shame and insecurity and hopelessness that I keep shut inside bursts through the gate like loosed demons. I don't hear their voices or feel their emotions until right around 3:30 in the morning, when they wake me up and torment me. They're irrational, and I tell them so, but in the darkness it doesn't matter. They're vestiges of childhood, and I tell them so, but again it doesn't matter. I toss and I turn, talking them back into their box inside my brain. It's been like this since I was about eight years old.

I'd rather endure the House of Pain during daylight, pushing my body to collapse and making it exhausted enough to sleep the night through, so I don't endure that alternate House of Pain at 3:30 in the morning. I need rest, and yet I fear rest.

I think a lot of us are like that, to differing degrees. I see it in the way people text while driving, find affirmation in the buzz of their iPhones, or choose the self-absorption of compulsive training over the connectedness of family. To know rest is to know quiet. To know quiet is to know a time without self-deception. And to know rest is also to know rejuvenation, as Vigil says. We become stronger.

Strength through rest. What a concept. It sounds like a slacker's manifesto. Or one of George Carlin's great oxymorons like "jumbo shrimp"—it can't be one *and* the other.

I want to be stronger. I want a Regeneration Timeframe that will make me powerful enough to quiet those irrational 3:30 a.m. voices.

"Sometimes," as Yves Montand tells James Garner in the John Frankenheimer racing film *Grand Prix,* "I get tired." To see that scene is to witness the exhausted strain behind the fading racing champion's eyes and to know that pushing himself to the brink is breaking him down, not making him stronger.

Not every moment of every day needs to be lived full tilt. I know this, but I don't yet model it for others. I want to know my mind and body well enough to back off before New Orleans syndrome shuts me down. I want to be the kind of guy who embraces the new slacker manifesto of strength through rest.

I'm just not there yet.

SUPERHEROES

My wife and I have subscribed to the Pacific Symphony's children's concerts since our boys were very young. What began as a well-intentioned effort to introduce them to fine classical music has become a tradition. It is a cherished constant in their lives, just like those familiar faces of the orchestra members, who have changed little over the years.

Each performance has a theme. Christmas, for example, is inevitably some variation on *The Nutcracker*. At some random point in the year, they bust out *Peter and the Wolf*. This morning's theme was superheroes. Movements from various superheroish symphonies were performed, everything from Tchaikovsky's *Romeo and Juliet Fantasy Overture* to John Williams's themes from *Star Wars* and *Superman March*. You have to be there to know the majesty of such moments. To hear a full orchestra tear into the *Raiders of the Lost Ark* theme is to live that old Neil Young axiom: "Live music is better, bumper stickers should be issued." I sit in our second-row seats and feel the music smash into my body. The complexity of each movement dazzles me. I find my creativity stirred, causing me to reach for a notebook and pen so I can write down the thoughts about story ideas and plot points that suddenly ricochet around my brainpan. It is a children's symphony—and yet it is not. On so many occasions over the years, the performances have moved me to tears. The music is transcendent, powerful, transformational. I sit there like a pile of mush, knowing quite well that I am sitting close enough for the orchestra to see this grown man crying. I don't care.

Another highlight of this morning's show was not only the playing of Michael Daugherty's *Metropolis Symphony* but the presence of the composer himself. Daugherty sat on stage, nodding to the music, and even closing his eyes and smiling at one passage. I marveled at such an opportunity. Writers don't often get the chance to see their work performed in front of an audience, and certainly not with the flair and spectacle of a live symphony. I found myself listening to the music but watching Daugherty. There's a wonderful moment in the writing process, when you read your *final* final polished draft before sending it to the publisher and you know in your gut that you've done it right. That's what I was watching up there.

During the final piece, Giachinno's *The Incredibles,* the giant video screen behind the orchestra flashed drawings of superheroes that members of the young audience had submitted prior to the show. They were childish and primitive. Most of the artists colored outside the jagged lines, which added to the charm. I saw Batman, Waterman, Spider-Man, and a bunch of surely parent-influenced newcomers like Doctor Man. I had a flashback to childhood and drawing stuff like that. I remembered my Batman lunchbox and my G.I. Joes and even the first time I saw *Star Wars.*

There's a reason for superheroes. For youngsters, they are the powerful, impervious images of ourselves we one day hope to become. They have muscles and wit and guile—and sometimes invisibility. Women love them. As we get older, superheroes get replaced by just plain heroes. For me, it was Steve Prefontaine. To Pre, America's great fallen distance legend, running was power and pride and guts, which spoke to me at a time in my life when I had none of that.

Later on I found nonrunning heroes, people like Hunter S. Thompson, Ernest Hemingway, and Bruce Springsteen. In their crafting of words and lyrics, I found inspiration to step outside my own middling way with the mother tongue and give my best sentences a pulse and beat that caused them to rise up off the page.

And then, inevitably, it happens. You find your own voice. I stepped on the backs of Hemingway and Thompson and even Pre to spin the words and build the attitude that became me. I no longer measured myself against them, because our paths diverged once I found that voice. My words and my running became deeply personal portrayals of who I am, warts and all. Not super. Not always heroic. But better, day by day, mile by mile, word by word. I will never write like Ernest Hemingway. Never ramble like Thompson. And never run like Pre. That doesn't mean I can't kick a little ass in my own inimitable fashion.

I left the symphony supercharged. On the way home, Callie and I stopped at a running store to buy new flats for Liam. The shop was crowded, but I was happy to wait. Put me in a gear store and I'm as content as the proverbial barnyard pig.

Within a few minutes, something started to bother me. It wasn't just the books and magazines they had for sale, which were connected by the common theme that running should be as mindless as possible. And it wasn't even the clerk who kept trying to push a brand of shoe that I considered substandard, but which I'm sure they overbought and needed to dump.

It was just the whole mood. Which was this: Running is mundane. Running is assembly line. Running can be boiled down to a business plan.

You need to know this about me: Running saved my life. Without running I would be dead somewhere. Just as Springsteen speaks of "the magic, the ministry, and the mystery of rock and roll," so I feel about running. It kept me sane when I was trying to find my way in life. It gave me a sense of self when the world didn't seem to get me. It gave me peace on days when my mind was chaos. It gave me glory as I crossed the finish line first. It gave me contentment, gave me connection, gave me catharsis.

It made me feel, on those days when the sun hit me just right, like a superhero.

But now running was just an act of commerce. To make matters worse, they sold Pre videos right next to books espousing mediocrity, status quo, and just good enough.

I bought Liam a spectacular pair of Asics and drove home in a snit. Calene kept looking at me as if I'd lost my mind. I'd gone from crying about superheroes and symphony composers to sniper-in-the-belfry within the span of thirty minutes.

My wife is a wonderful woman who knows me well. These were her words: *You need to go for a run.*

Bruising rains had wreaked havoc on Southern California. My trails were underwater and muddy. But I needed the solitude of the wilderness, so I set out during a lull in the storms. I sloshed through mud and water for four miles before breaking brush onto the local golf course. It's a little known fact that golf courses are the best places to run on a rainy day, because they're built for optimal drainage. So while the golfers themselves stayed home, I had the most perfect little cross-country course in Orange County all to myself.

There's always that *moment* on an angry run day. It comes about thirty minutes in. As I trotted down the thirteenth fairway, past three deer standing in the rough and eyeing me as if unsure whether I was friend or hunter, the moment hit. Here it was: I was the problem. The folks at the running store were just doing their jobs. They were selling shoes and shirts and shorts and books and magazines and watches and socks and pretty much everything else to a group of people who were mostly nonrunners. They were bored and irritable and tired of silly questions, just like any employee at any store. But they were handing out the keys to the kingdom. All those shoes and shirts and other stuff were the uniforms of superheroes. If I'd said it out loud in the store, people would have thought I was nuts. But when those same folks cross the finish line of their first marathon or 10-K or any race that demands their very best, I guarantee you they will feel like superheroes.

That's what running does to lives. It's not just exercise. It's not just achievement. It's a daily discipline that has nothing to do with speed, weight, social status, sexual orientation, political affiliation, where you live, what car you drive, or whether anyone anywhere loves you. It's about the slow and painful process of being the best you can be. That's why the first step out the door is always so hard. That's when we choose between settling for average and being a superhero version of ourselves.

Some days, average wins.

But man, when you go superhero . . .

THUNDER THIGHS

Photos of me finishing the Disneyland Marathon show rivers of blood coursing down my inner thighs. The day had begun cool and pleasant, but as the race completed its first 13.1-mile loop around the Magic Kingdom, the sun became intense. Mild Santa Ana winds sucked all the moisture from the air, turning the morning desert dry. Making matters worse, race organizers had misplaced course markers early in the race, shortening the course by a half-mile or so. They made the command decision to fix the problem by tacking the missing mileage on to the end of the course.

Now, we all know how tough it is to measure something as simple as a local running loop. You get in the car, you punch the odometer to zero, then you drive the loop very cautiously and carefully, hoping to approximate the exact distance. Variables like turning radius enter the equation, perhaps adding a few feet here and there. In the end, what you get is a close guesstimate of the actual distance. You do not, even under the most particular and persnickety of measurements, achieve the precision of a measuring wheel that clicks off each and every precise inch traveled. But it doesn't matter, right? Because this is just your local loop, and the world does not hinge on whether it's longer or shorter than what you think it might be. Your personal record on this course is actually the world record, and that's all that matters.

Anyway, the Disney folks decided to remeasure the course. During the race. Through Disneyland. The park was open, and thousands of tourists were thronging about. And the backstage areas where the new mileage would be added were almost as busy with cast members, as Disney calls their employees. I didn't see the people who did the remeasurement, and perhaps no one saw the people who did the remeasurement. I have a sneaking suspicion that there was no remeasurement but, instead, a best guess at what constituted that missing mileage. Don't get me wrong: I'm a big fan of Disneyland and am fond of making the short drive up the 5 Freeway to make liberal use of my annual pass.

But on that day, somewhere between mile twenty and mile twenty-eight—because I'm pretty sure that's how far my "marathon" ended up being—my love for all things Disney cooled. I slipped from a 2:51 pace to a 3:01-and-change without altering my tempo or my stride all that much. We ran forever in that backstage area, seeing a rather mundane and uninteresting side of Disneyland that a lifelong fan such as myself would quite rather have skipped, thank you very much.

The final stretch was out of that abyss into the throngs of the park itself. The course followed the parade route from its gate at Small World to the Matterhorn and then down Main Street. Thousands of people lined the route, and the announcer yelled my name as I crossed the line. He even knew that I'd done a little writing and made sure to let the audience know. So I felt special, even if I did feel gypped out of my 2:51.

But the blood . . .

Nobody had seen fit to add an aid station to our new loops, at least none that I saw. So I stopped sweating. Everywhere. The Santa Ana winds blasted me with their hot gusts, drying any vestige of water on my body. This is not something you sense immediately from a wetness or dryness point of view. Rather, it takes the form of gnawing pain. First it is the chafing that comes when dry skin under the arms rubs raw the dry skin of the arms themselves. This problem is easily solved—simply separate the arms from the body while running. It doesn't matter that you look like a turkey or one of those runners who overrotate the upper body as they run, taking on the appearance of C-3PO.

The inner thighs are a different story. Step by step, they rub against each other. The pain starts as a nuisance and soon becomes unbearable. I have tried many ways of stopping this chafing: pulling my shorts down lower so that the fabric rubs against itself, applying spit as a stop-gap lubricant (only lasts a few seconds and somehow makes the pain worse), and even dousing my loins with water. None of them work.

Sometimes this chafing comes about because of the Santa Ana winds and a lack of moisture. Sometimes it comes from too *much* moisture—when an overly long run produces shorts saturated in sweat, which then becomes an irritant. Sometimes it just happens because I've gained a few pounds, and no force on earth can stop my chubby little quads from creating enough friction to start a campfire. Right now I'm struggling with a daily ration of these nuisances because I'm carrying a little extra beef. The obvious manner of stopping them is to use a good lubricant or wear compression shorts under my running apparel. (Not a bad idea, but the seams all come together at a rather pivotal point, causing a hellishly terrifying chafing on a part of my anatomy that does not now—nor will it ever—need a good chafing.)

But what sort of lubricant? I read somewhere long ago that Vaseline is not a good choice, though I can't really remember why. And I used something called Sports Slick at the Raid Gauloises a few years back. It worked really well, though I'm not sure they make it anymore. I guess the real issue in this case isn't the type of lubricant but being willing to admit that you are carrying enough extra tonnage to warrant a good lube job. I can look at myself in the mirror ten different ways, trying to find the angle that will convince me I am thin. Once I find that angle, I can literally think thin. It's a positive thought process that makes me feel sleek and fast, so I disregard any hint that I require a substance to decrease the Kelvin reading between my legs.

The self-delusion continues as I convince myself that I like the challenge of beating the chafe. I try not to overpronate, I open up my stride, I make sure to wear shorts with an inseam longer than two inches, and—voilà! Yes, I'm vain. And I'm certainly dumb to invite the pain of midrun and postrun chafing. But we all have our methods, and part of my running formula is to leave the house with a minimalist kit—nothing more on my body than a pair of shoes, a pair of socks, a pair of shorts, and a shirt. If I am thin—or so far out in the wilderness that no one can see me—the shirt becomes optional. I don't carry water bottles, I don't wear hydration packs, and I don't slather gooey pitch all over the tops of my legs. I am a runner, not a Channel swimmer.

Back to Disneyland. I hobbled to the end of the finish chute, walking with my legs so far apart that I looked like it had been my turn in the barrel. Even that didn't do any good, because by that point it was literally impossible to prevent my legs from rubbing against each other. So I just endured it, blood and all, even as people literally looked away in horror (or could not look away, depending upon their constitution). This endurance took on the form of its own marathon as I wandered aimlessly about the Magic Kingdom in search of my bride. Calene was nowhere to be found, and when we finally did connect, it was another mile of walking back to our hotel.

The legs scabbed a day later, as they will. And for four solid days I wore compression shorts around the clock, painful privates chafing be hanged.

So what's the point of this story? The point is that I'm not complaining. Sometimes when you run, things hurt. It's easy to get dewy-eyed about an endorphin rush or a twilight jog along the hard sand at high tide, but pain and suffering are equally powerful aspects of running's transformational power. That hurt is sometimes the thing that makes you feel like the day was worth getting out of bed. It's the sear in your lungs at the top of a hard climb, the blister you ignore for mile after mile, the toenail that has chosen to secede from the body. And it's the thighs, those hulking emissaries that churn and churn and churn, burning and bleeding and rubbing themselves raw like beluga scraping off their skin in the Arctic shallows.

The pain is temporary. Memories of the perseverance last forever.

"I delight," Paul wrote in his second letter to the Corinthians, "in weaknesses, in insults, in hardships, in persecutions, in difficulties. For when I am weak, then I am strong."

THE RUNNER'S
WORLD

PAMPLONA (PART 1)

"Did you have a hard time finding white pants?" asked my buddy Ron, a Delta 767 captain. It was the day after the Fourth of July. Ron and I had flown from Los Angeles, cleared customs in Madrid, and were now driving to Pamplona with three of Ron's flying buddies in a rented micro-van—five grown men squeezed into a car designed for waif models. The Spanish countryside was sweltering, golden and spare. It looked like the central coast of California, I thought, predevelopment.

"White pants?"

"For the run. It's tradition." Ron briefed me on the uniform. During the Festival of San Fermín—when the *encierro*, or running of the bulls, is just one of many folkloric activities—Pamplona becomes a city apart from the rest of the world, complete with its own rituals and garb. Everyone wears white pants and shirt, a red sash, and a red kerchief. Everyone but the police. They wear blue and scowl as if Franco was still in power.

"I guess I can buy them when we get there."

"I brought an extra pair, just in case. You can borrow them if you want."

Ron's a great guy. I didn't want to embarrass him in front of his friends by pointing out the vast disparities in our girths. It's not that he was heavy or even stout. In fact, Ron is a perfectly fit, well-proportioned guy. But I had been a runner all my life. In my mind's eye, I am still the same skinny kid with the long blond hair who ran NCAA cross-country. I imagined that his pants would be so baggy on me that it would be like wearing a circus clown's clothes. A clear mental image of trying to outrace a bull in Ron's pants appeared. The pants kept dropping to my ankles as the bull prepared to commit one of those signature Pamplona moments—the one that begins with penetration by a horn tip and ends with the runner getting hurled into the air like a rag doll. "That's okay," I said, cheeks taut. "I'll see if I can find a pair."

By midafternoon we made Pamplona. The city was listing, an unwieldy vessel swamped by the biggest public drunk this side of a weeklong Jimmy Buffett concert. The cobbled streets thronged with revelers: backpackers of a dozen nationalities, Eurotrash with their spike-collared dogs, hordes of pale-legged tourists drawn by curiosity. Those with money perched on wicker chairs at marble-topped café tables, drinking cold ale and *calimochos* under the hot July sun. Budget travelers sprawled on the ground or milled about the town square, passing around gallon jugs of red wine. Street guitarists turned their miniature amplifiers up to eleven. Coeds perched on their boyfriends' shoulders. Aging men with white beards preened in the bustling cafés, their flitting eyes betraying a deep longing that some passerby exclaim how that old guy over there looks just like Hemingway.

There were two constants, though, bringing us thousands together. First was the question. "Are you running?" was repeated in every conversation, in every language. It buzzed through the air like a good rumor, reminding us all why we'd traveled so far. It certainly wasn't for the opportunity to wear the Pamplona uniform.

Which brings me to the second constant: Everyone was wearing the uniform.

"We look out of place," I said to Ron. The sun was burning the back of my neck. "Why don't you go change while I do some shopping."

"No need to shop. You can borrow those extra pants of mine," he reminded me as a squadron of Italian women sashayed past, saucy and hip like supermodels on furlough. They made the uniform look salacious. They could have made a coat of armor look salacious.

"I'd hate to ruin your pants," I said.

So we went shopping. I bought a simple white T-shirt in a small store off the plaza. It was poorly made, inexpensive, and disposable—exactly what I wanted. I procured the red sash and neckerchief from street vendors. All this took ten minutes. But I could not find white pants. Not that I was picky: denim, polyester, cotton, or spandex; bell-bottoms, pleated, or matador. They would have all suited me fine. I wanted white pants with a thirty-two-inch waist and a proportional inseam. Nothing more. Surely, in a city of nearly two hundred thousand well-dressed people, such a garment existed.

The shopping continued. Photographs of leviathan bulls were plastered on store windows. Their necks were massive coils of muscle whose function reminded me of a lion's forearm I saw once on the Tanzanian savannah—a weapon, not a body part. Each bull's horns drew to natural, lethal points. The theme of several window collages was runners being gored. Death is a very real possibility at the encierro. Fourteen runners have died since 1924, and hundreds more have been injured. One haunting photograph shows a skinny little man impaled on the horns of a bull. The man is helpless, his flaccid torso draped about the bull's neck like a mink stole, about to be shrugged to the heavens. I began to get nervous.

By sundown the shops were all closing. I still hadn't found white pants. "Maybe I can run in jeans," I said.

"Really, I don't mind if you borrow them. You can even ruin them for all I care. They're extra."

We'd had a few beers. It was time to be honest. "I don't think they're gonna fit, Ron. And I didn't bring a belt."

"They should fit just fine. They're a thirty-six."

Poor Ron. He was such a bad judge of fitness. "I'm a thirty-two, Ron." Even that sounded large.

There is a wonderful tact to Ron Allen. A grace and diplomacy I do not possess. He merely gave me a curious look—raising an eyebrow, so to speak, without actually raising it—but said nothing. Just then the other pilots found us. They were all wearing the uniform. In our jeans and colored T-shirts, Ron and I looked as out of place as two guys wearing black tie and tails to a NASCAR race. "Let's go to the bullfight."

Our seats were in the upper tier of the circular Plaza de Toros coliseum. The crowd was littered with tourists. Most of the audience, however, was Spaniards. Their knowledge and passion about bullfighting was powerful. They did not see it as sport, for it clearly was not. Instead, they viewed bullfighting as a means of artistic expression—an extreme and mildly absurd form, but a form nonetheless. Equal parts raucous and refined, wedged tightly onto the narrow bench seats but reveling in the warm summer night and preperformance expectation, they could just as easily have been a crowd on the lawn at the Hollywood Bowl, waiting for the Los Angeles Philharmonic to play Beethoven.

The ritual of the bullfight, like a symphony, began with an overture. The bull was released into the arena and greeted by that staccato burst of applause that greets a conductor when he appears from the wings to stand before his orchestra. The bull appeared surprised and disoriented. He made great circles around the dirt floor, giant neck rippling and hooves pounding, acclimating himself. Each bull, it is said, seeks a place of sanctuary in the arena. This is the place he will return to again and again during a bullfight to regain his strength.

Meanwhile, the matador introduced himself by marching onto the arena's hard-packed dirt floor. He was accompanied by his assistants, the *banderilleros*, wearing capes of pink and gold. The bull and matador sized one another up from a distance. Then the matador and banderilleros departed, leaving the bull alone to wonder, no doubt, what the hell was going on.

He didn't have long to wonder. The first act began immediately. A lone picador galloped into the arena on horseback. His job was to anger and weaken the bull by thrusting short lances into those mighty neck muscles. This caused the animal's head to lower, leading to a more focused charge. Several times over the course of that evening's bullfights, the picadors and their blinkered steeds were nearly gored. Only the telepathy between horse and rider allowed them to prance away in the nick of time.

The second act belonged to the banderilleros. The three of them returned after the picador had gone about his business. They attempted to further weaken the bull by thrusting colorful barbed sticks into its neck. Brave but not artistic, the banderilleros flitted about the bull like gnats, prancing in close to inflict their pain, make him angry, make him tired. I admired their courage but was rooting for the bull. The great animal, so noble and fierce, was better than them.

By the time the matador entered the arena for the *suerte de matar* (death act), the bull was in a state of bewildered rage. The matador and his flimsy red cape were alone with the animal. The matador's goal was to plunge a sword straight down between the bull's shoulders into its heart. At this point the bull's goal would be not so much staying alive as killing the matador.

The audience had come to see neither bull nor matador destroyed. Unlike a soccer match or horse race, they were less interested in the outcome than the artistry necessary to achieve it—the journey as opposed to the destination. It was certainly different from the billfish tournament I covered off Kona one year. The sight of a majestic silver-blue swordfish ("the lions of the ocean") being gaffed in the name of sport lacked any sense of the aesthetic or any significant risk to the fishermen.

The Spaniards cheered equally for man and bull throughout the night, though cowardly matadors were barely tolerated. Even the most refined women could be seen whispering to one another scornfully, rolling their eyes about the man in the arena's waning or absolutely nonexistent talent. The best bulls and best matadors, on the other hand, were showered with glory. Applause and cheers ricocheted around the ancient coliseum like reflected beams of sunshine.

Good or bad, cowardly or brave, no one took their eyes off the matador. He was doing something beyond the spectator's ken, risking their wrath and his own life in an attempt to do something bold, uncomfortable, and ultimately glorious. In a world so often defined by mediocrity, he was pushing himself in a way the crowd subconsciously longed to emulate. I couldn't look away.

No one in that vast arena could. I was struck by the thought that my own life, despite attempts to suffuse it with some semblance of personal excellence, repeatedly strayed down that path of mediocrity. I settled for good enough instead of striving to be my very best.

I vowed to change that, some way, somehow.

A RUNNER'S WORLD

It is the last Sunday morning in July. I arrived in Paris well past midnight, exhausted from the long drive north. The Rue de Rivoli was a madhouse, thick with tourists and revelers. I checked in and walked around for an hour to find a meal, but nothing was open. After settling for peanuts and a cold Leffe at a bistro on the Rue de la Madeleine, I hit the sack. There was no thought of a wake-up call.

It is my ritual in Paris to rise early and run along the Seine. I like the solitude of the early hour; the sifting and sorting of emotions that comes with a workout so far from home, in a city so historical and magnificent, on paths trod for centuries by peasants, soldiers, students, whores, merchants, musketeers, kings, tourists— and now runners.

But it is close to noon as I step outside my hotel. The last Sunday in July is also known to Parisians as the last day of the Tour de France. Police barricades separate street from sidewalk throughout the heart of Paris, lining the route the Tour will follow this afternoon—and blocking my access to the Seine. The sidewalks are jammed with spectators saving their viewing spots, making it impossible to walk more than a few steps without stopping to squeeze through the congestion. Running is out of the question.

This is clearly a time for extreme measures.

I head back to my room.

One great perk of being a journalist at the Tour is the press credential. It not only allows access to the riders and teams, but also makes it possible to step over the barricades and onto the course itself. An ordinary spectator attempting the same maneuver would promptly be arrested.

I've been covering the bike race for three weeks, following it from city to city as it wound around France. Now, I grab my credential off the nightstand. Holding the stiff 3 x 5 piece of laminated plastic in my hand, I plunge into the crowds until I am once more pressed against a barricade. A blue-uniformed gendarme stands on the other side, arms crossed. I flash my credential, not sure whether the same rules about course access apply in frenzied Paris.

They do.

The policeman waves his hand and nods at me like we are instant friends. He beckons me to climb over. I swing one leg across the barricade, then another.

And then I am on the course, a lone runner on a broad empty boulevard, surrounded on all sides by chaos and crowds on the other side of the barricades. I break into a steady run up the sycamore-lined Champs-Élysées. There are no cars, no motorcycles. Just me. The road climbs gently toward the Arc de Triomphe. Pavement was laid over its cobblestones after protesters famously hurled them at police in 1968. But here and there the blacktop is thin, and the ancient cobbles poke through.

I'm not much on runners who call attention to themselves—"stunt running," I call it. These are the self-promoters who shout to the world about their fifty marathons in fifty days, or basically can't step out for a run without calling a publicist.

My drug of choice is solitude. My favorite runs take place without a single eyewitness. But today is different. There are no trails in Paris, and no place to run but the actual Tour de France course. Unwilling or not, I have made myself a center of attention.

I lope past the Hôtel de Crillon and then up the Champs, with its trendy boutiques, jam-packed cafes, and that little dirt walkway under the row of sycamores where I snapped a picture of my wife on a brisk October afternoon two years ago.

In the framed photograph, Calene looks beautiful and serene, her lips and cheeks flushed from a sharp wind, bundled in an overcoat and gray scarf. Her smile is that of the Mona Lisa. She was tired. We had walked miles that day and the sun was setting. Soon we would stop for *un pichet* of white wine and salade Niçoise with great hunks of bread and butter. But first, as the autumn sun began to disappear, I took a photograph. It is my favorite Paris moment.

I run on.

Not so many years ago, the sight of a man running for no reason whatsoever would have seemed an act of lunacy—or larceny. It's safe to assume that running up the Champs-Élysées on the final Sunday in July would also entail being stopped by the police and politely questioned about the motivation for this odd behavior. "Why are you running?" "What are you running from?" I can hear it now. A lone runner would have been no different than a man in a clown costume riding a unicycle.

Times have changed. Running as reverie is no longer absurd. But back when I first began thinking of myself as a runner in the early 1970s, the sport was a secret society, misunderstood by the general populace. Runners were taunted on the roads by wolf whistles and cheers of "pick it up," and puzzled by the unplumbed mysteries of a proper training diet (I consistently fueled up with Ding-Dongs, Hostess Fruit Pies, and glazed Winchell's Donuts). Back then, when shoes and shorts made just for running did not exist, I trained in cotton T-shirts, thick BX tube socks, and canvas Pro-Keds. A typical race entry fee was five dollars. Instead of electronic computer chips to record finish time and place, wooden tongue depressors were handed out at the finish line, each with a number in black Magic Marker denoting finish spot. "1" for first place, "2" for second, and so on.

It was a small world, clubby and homespun, limited in my mind to the running bastions of America and Britain. There was a special magazine for people like us. The subject matter of *Runner's World* wasn't the "world" in the broader context, but that very small bubble known as the running community. In this way, it was like its niche sister publications *Camping World* and *Scuba World*, pulling the reader inward to the wonders of our secret society, shutting out the actual world at large.

Running has since exploded (one could argue the same for

camping and scuba, though not in the same numbers). The world of running—the runner's world, so to speak—is now universal. More people run than do any other sport. Everyone runs or knows someone who does. Marathons are contested on each of the seven continents.

The mindset of the modern runner has expanded accordingly. In ever growing numbers, runners are taking the simple sport they practice in humble ritualistic fashion on the roads and trails of their hometown, and transport themselves thousands of miles to do it somewhere else. "Destination running"—the practice of seeing the planet by traveling to far-flung endurance races—is now a tent pole of the tourism industry.

In this way, runners are modern explorers, venturing into parts of the world they do not know as part of their travel experience, while at the same time pushing their bodies into uncharted realms of discomfort and stamina during the race itself, hoping to discover a new and more empowered version of themselves.

What brought this about? The nature of the sport has changed, with less emphasis on elite competition and more on participation. It is the true bastion of the Olympic ideal put forth by Pierre de Coubertin: "The important thing in the Olympic Games is not to win, but to take part; the important thing in life is not triumph, but the struggle; the essential thing is not to have conquered but to have fought well."

This does not completely explain the grown men who run half-marathons in half-naked costumes as Princess Leia or Mary Poppins, but it's a start. Finishing is more important than winning.

Women, who used to be forbidden from taking part for fear their reproductive organs would slip from their bodies after too many footfalls, now make up a majority of the community.

Now, more than ever before, running belongs to everyone.

Yet running is still a uniquely individual experience. Each person's daily run is singular unto themselves, no matter whether they are racing alongside 35,000 strangers at the London Marathon each year in April—or me, jogging alone up the Champs-Élysées in July because I need a proper sweat and there is nowhere else to run.

At the exact spot in front of the Arc de Triomphe where the riders will make a complete 180-degree turn seven hours from now, I step back over the barricades and off the course, on my way to take a leisurely running tour of Paris. I have crossed from one side of the city to the other, thanks to my credential. Now it is time to leave the Champs.

The sun is beating down and the tourists are everywhere—the Louvre, Musée d'Orsay, Notre Dame. The lines to climb the steps of the Eiffel Tower are so long that enormous wind machines blow mist onto the throngs, lest someone pass out from heat exhaustion.

I finish my run by flashing my credential to hop back over the barricades one last time, then sprint across the Place de la Concorde to my hotel. Any other day of the year and this hub is a traffic jam. Today it is just me. The moment is surreal. I have neither conquered nor triumphed, though I have definitely struggled.

This is not my favorite Paris moment. That will forever belong to Callie posing beneath the sycamores along the Champs.

But it is second.

That's the way it is in the runner's world. Each run becomes a memory that can instantly transport us anywhere. Running is an interaction with a city, a street, a trail, the smell of the air, the blazing heat; the drizzle, the nausea, the deep humidity, the wind in our face that makes us feel like we're running in slow motion, and the painful horror of that time it felt as if there was absolutely, positively no way of finding a bathroom in time to stop the unthinkable from happening. I can instantly recall the memories of that golf course run in Kota Kinabalu, the morning along the Thames, that bitter cold surge along the Tokyo waterfront, that December afternoon in Prague, the grass loops next to the crashing surf of the North Shore, and the favorite trail around Rancho I've run a thousand times. Those courses and sensations stay with you always, a virtual reality tour of the runner's world hardwired into our brains. Because running is the only sport you can do anywhere, at any time, without having to look for a ball or a pool or rent clubs, or even enough players to constitute a team.

You just run.

Even more than ten years later, the memory of that run around Paris on the last day of the Tour de France in 2005 transports me to the Champs-Élysées every time I think of it. I sweat in the warm July air, see the sunglasses and espresso demitasse of tourists sitting at metal-topped café tables, sense the cobbles beneath my feet, and the vastness of sudden open space as I run beneath the Eiffel Tower into the tree-lined Champ de Mars.

The memory will be there as long as I live.

THE WILD PLACE

From a runner's point of view, Pulau Tiga doesn't offer much in the way of diversity. At just three miles long and a mile wide, this island two hours by fast boat off the coast of Borneo is an impossible place to cobble together a ten-miler. The thin swatch of white sand ringing the jungle is broken up at both ends of the island by jagged rocks forming an obstacle to circumnavigation. And that thick carpet of trees and vines covering the middle is crisscrossed by only a handful of narrow game trails thanks to monitor lizards.

But I am a curious sort. I believe that nothing clears the mind like a trail run and that a trail can be found almost anywhere. With a trail comes adventure, quiet, and the joy of going rogue. So I made a few tentative forays into the jungle of Pulau Tiga during my stay there, stumbling into dead ends and running in small circles. The trails were wispy and almost overgrown, trod by small animals instead of pressed down by repeated human incursion. Paths like that are frustrating. They meander without purpose or destination. Five steps this way, four steps that, leading you on for a couple of miles or maybe just a couple of yards.

One trail stopped cold at the edge of a vast muck. I couldn't see across to the other side, so the swamp might have gone on for hundreds of yards. I tiptoed around the fringes of the mud and decay, feeling the oppressive darkness of the jungle canopy forming a claustrophobic bond with the soupy floor. There was no sound. Even the air felt dead.

Suddenly, a great chill raced down my spine. It was a moment of instant and unexplained terror. I sprinted back to the sea. Gulping the briny air, I reveled in the breeze and the lack of trees or branches pressing down on me. That white sand may have been a boring place to run, but just then it seemed most ideal indeed.

Before I could trot back to the little yellow tent just off the beach that I was calling home for six weeks, a local botanist stopped me. "You shouldn't do that," he said, looking very Zen.

"I like to get in a few miles every day," I told him, not really quite sure why he was bothering me. I thought he was talking about running.

"No. You shouldn't go in the jungle. Especially that part of the jungle." Whereupon my new hero possibly saved my life by telling me about the 30-foot-long reticulated pythons who make a habit of dropping out of the treetops, knocking their prey unconscious, then wrapping them up and eating them. Apparently, Pulau Tiga was once home to herds of wild pigs. The pythons have wiped them out.

If pythons were able to unhinge their jaws enough to eat a corpulent pig, they were certainly capable of doing the same to me. This fact was reinforced after my return home, thanks to a Discovery

Channel special showing frightening video of a python eating a man not far from Pulau Tiga. (In case you're interested, the snakes work top to bottom, knowing that once they get past the shoulders there are no more broad, bony body parts to hamper complete ingestion.)

I confined my runs to the beach after that, though never after sunset, when the poisonous sea snakes are said to crawl onto land to feast on the rodent population. But as soon as I flew back home, I resumed running on trails. The canyon less than three minutes from my home is a spectacular wilderness of sycamore and oaks, riven by a single great stream that either dries up in summer or rages as a furious and muddy river at high flood. Not a run goes by when I don't appreciate the smell of dried grass or the cactus flowers so purple and yellow, or even just the horrible crimson beauty of poison oak during autumn. My skin gets itchy just looking at it, as if the stuff might jump out at me. Sometimes, when I'm all swollen and bubbly skinned from an outbreak, I'm sure that it has.

I should add that not a run goes by when I'm not looking out for mountain lions, bobcats, coyotes, and rattlesnakes. I've seen them all down there. And the scary thing is that I am sure they have seen me far more often. Last summer, in the final miles of a hot August run, I was running too close to the edge of the trail. Rattlesnakes like to camouflage themselves in the leaves and grass there, waiting for the best possible moment to slither across without birds of prey spotting them. This particular rattlesnake wanted no part of me. Coiled and poised to strike, it shook its rattles two steps before I would have stepped on its head. My standard fright response is to leap high in the air and scream like a little girl—which is exactly what I did.

I have surprised a black bear and her two cubs on the Rock Trail in Mammoth, wandered into the midst of mighty elk in Jackson, surprised a moose in the Rockies, and on one surreal Sierra run, found myself surrounded by a herd of deer that stood stone still, trying to convince me they weren't there. That's what deer do in danger situations. They freeze, no matter how incredibly weird this hiding in plain sight might appear. I froze, too. And while I had many miles to run and a pressing need to complete them in a short period of time, I forgot my hurry. One doe finally broke the spell by creeping stealthily in the opposite direction. This was the signal for the others to follow. It was like watching a congregation sneak out of church in the middle of the sermon, eyes downcast, slightly embarrassed that anyone might be looking at them. Only when they were safely away did those deer bound into the distance.

As you can guess, those encounters with wildlife add immeasurably to my runs. To see a box turtle or roadrunner or hawk in the wild is far better than in some zoo. To that point, I should admit that I refrained from running when I was crossing the African savannah a few years back. It's one thing to run through wilderness. It's another thing entirely to feel that primal tang of the tall grass and acacias, knowing any number of predators are hidden within, waiting for some fool like me.

Thing is, my trail is no different. A few years back, a mountain biker was attacked and killed by a mountain lion near my canyon.

My friend Austin Murphy was in town a couple of days later, doing a *Sports Illustrated* story about the tragedy. We ran to the site and saw where the attack had taken place. Saw the path where the lion had dragged the body through a thicket of cactus and thorns to hide it from other predators. It was as spooky as you can imagine, and I have never run that trail again. I also never crouch down to tie my shoes in the wild since then, as that would make me look smaller and more preylike. The mountain biker was apparently bending down to fix a broken chain when the attack occurred.

A friend who spends as much time as I do on trails recently told me of a mountain lion sighting. He'd seen it with his own eyes, strolling through the tall grass near where the sheriffs busted the big marijuana farm a couple of years back. That spot happens to be smack in the middle of one of my favorite loops. Yet I haven't run down there since I heard about the big cat.

Eventually I will. At some point I'll convince myself that the threat is no more—or at least reduced. Some whim will command me to go right instead of left at the crossroads under the bridge, and a mile later I will be running through that path by the former pot plantation. The drug bust was so astounding because the vegetation is so thick that no one knew about the acres of towering green plants growing among the bamboo along the stream. Still, a big cat is even more easily hidden.

So why take the risk? When I'm on the trails, my mind is free. The absolute quiet is a haven, broken only by the whoosh of the wind, the jackhammer pounding of a woodpecker, and the frantic rustle of squirrels sprinting through dried leaves. Being in nature challenges me, fills me with a sense of adventure, and makes me whole. I feel the weather more keenly, be it plodding through mud and raindrops or tanning the back of my neck in the scorching sun. My senses are heightened. If the trail leads to the top of a commanding hill, I feel my cares slip away with each step of the climb until I stand on top, above it all, energized by the view and the effort it took to get there.

Only on a trail.

On those trails, nagging riddles and problems have a way of uncomplicating themselves, revealing to me in step-by-step detail how they might be resolved. Or, at the very least, why they're not as calamitous as they might appear. One habit I have is to go into my office first thing in the morning to work, and then go for a run when I've written myself into a corner. Sometimes it just takes a few hundred yards on the sanctuary of a trail for a new sentence or paragraph to write itself in my head, gently guiding me out of that corner and back into the story I was meant to write.

But most of all, I seek out trails because the hardest packed dirt is always softer than pavement, the scent of sage and licorice beats breathing exhaust any day of the week, and once in every great while, I witness some natural marvel that makes me high with wonder. Right now I am thinking of a hot afternoon atop Chiquita Ridge, a wide rutted path that falls away for a few hundred feet on either side. A pair of red-tailed hawks had found a thermal wind system pushing up the incline. They took turns riding that thermal, gliding low over the valley floor, then folding their wings back as the current shot them like rockets up and over the ridgeline, holding their aerodynamic tuck until they ran out of wind and were about to stall and plummet back to earth. Only then would they open their broad wings and wheel back down into the valley and do it all again.

To make the most of the current, they were flying just ten feet from the slope. Their bodies made an audible whoosh as they blasted past me up into the spotless blue sky. I stood stone still, an enthralled would-be Icarus. Never have I felt a lack of wings with more envy.

Hawks at play. The only place I could have seen something so sublime and utterly cool is on a trail.

I feel like I am tempting fate by writing about this. And while I will be vigilant at all times and not do anything reckless when it comes to running through wilderness (and it is wilderness, despite the tract homes sprouting just a few hundred yards away), I can't see myself staying away from the trails. I don't have a death wish, but as much as I love to run, if I can't do it on trails, I'd rather not do it at all.

With that choice comes risk. I am aware of it. The winter after wildfire raged up the slopes of Saddleback Mountain, that benevolent giant looming out my back window, my good friend Jamie rode his mountain bike to the summit. The land had been scorched completely. He rode through the charred remains of what had once been a sweeping forest of manzanita and scrub oak, smelling only ash and seeing no signs of life. Something large caught his eye on the slope, and he got off his bike to look. There, entwined in a small hole, were dozens of the biggest and fattest rattlers any of us would ever want to see. Just to make sure people would believe him, he took a picture. It is awesome and terrifying.

Rattlesnakes are territorial. That slithering mass of hibernation would have been hidden by vegetation any other year—and soon will be once again. Imagine the runner who chooses to deviate off course and has the bad luck to stumble into that small hole.

Actually, I'd rather not. To run the wilderness is to say a small prayer that God will protect you. When I was just fourteen and living near the banks of the American River, I would escape the house for long runs. My dad was in Vietnam that year, and our house could be a crazy place. Those runs were my escape.

Shorter than five feet and just eighty pounds, I was a vulnerable target for whatever might be lurking out there. So I developed this obsessive-compulsive prayer that covered all possible problems, legalities, and loopholes: "Dear God, I pray that I am not attacked and/or molested while participating in, and/or competing in, any kinds of activity. I pray that I am not bitten by a snake and/or any other kind of animal. And I pray that I do not get a stitch—you know, a pain in my side—while participating in, and/or competing in, any kind of activity."

That is the prayer of a child, putting on the mental armor that will bestow an illusory cloak of safety. As loopy as that prayer might read, I find those words popping up out of my subconscious even today. Part of me is still very much that towheaded little fourteen-year-old who used the wilderness to escape and find himself at the same time. To enter that wilderness, or any wilderness, is a leap of faith.

It's a leap I make almost every day. And I find myself out there, even now.

PAMPLONA (PART II)

Seven. Sun just up. I walked with Ron and the pilots down an alley built before Columbus discovered the New World. None of us had gotten more than two hours' sleep. Too much excitement. Too many bodies swaying in the streets; sometimes dancing as couples, more often not. The warm night air had smelled of sweat and expensive perfume. By the time we stumbled off to bed, the town was just kicking into that partying mode reserved for true professionals. Even the pilots, who treated revelry as a birthright, were wrung out.

In the morning the cobbled streets and narrow medieval alleys were puddled with red wine, vomit, and pools of urine so vast they could have been considered estuaries or lakes and given their own geographical place names. Thick green shards of broken glass rose from the vile puddles. The march from our hotel to the run course was like tiptoeing through a minefield.

For all those sensations, what had me reeling were the white pants I wore—the *tight* white pants. Borrowed from Ron, they clung to my thighs like sausage skins. It had been a struggle to button the waist.

Sometimes it's a major event that provides the impetus for change. Say, the death of a close relative. Sometimes it's something considerably smaller, like being confronted with a forty-pound weight gain moments before being chased down a narrow, crowded, wine-sticky, piss-slippery stretch of cobblestones by a half-ton killing machine.

I remembered a moment the year before, standing at the head-waters of the Yangtze River while covering an adventure race. "So, Martin," asked a longtime Chinese colleague with typical cultural directness, "when did you get the belly?"

And there was that book signing during the summer thunder-storm in Albuquerque, when the Borders manager took one look at me and chuckled, "You sure don't look like your author photo."

My answer to both was the same: I've been lifting. It's muscle.

This officially marked the second time I had gotten fat. So, no, I wasn't the skinny blond kid who ran NCAA cross-country any-more. That much I could deal with. The weight gain didn't trouble me as much as what it implied. Careerwise, I was pushing myself to be my best. But in all other areas of life—family, appearance, fitness, spirituality—the desire to be my best had imperceptibly been replaced by a lowering of standards. And I couldn't explain why. The dissipation of Pamplona and my physical appearance were not mirror reflections. They were close enough to the truth, though, to sting.

My ruminations came to an end as we reached a high wooden barricade near the Plaza Consistorial. It was the moment of deci-sion. On the other side were the runners, awaiting the 8 a.m.

release of the bulls. On our side were spectators and would-be runners in a cloud of second thoughts. I climbed over. Ron and the other pilots clambered up the rails, too.

The tightly packed scrum inside the barricades was claustrophobic. The street was so narrow, and the sea of red and white so great, that there was no room to move. I can't imagine what would have happened if the bulls had been released at that moment.

Lowering my shoulders, I forced my way down Mercaderes Street into the heart of the mob. Apartment buildings rose three stories up on either side, casting us in shadow, like an urban slot canyon. Spectators looked down with bemusement from balconies. I twisted my neck to look behind me and realized I had lost Ron and the others. When I didn't see them after a moment standing on my tiptoes, I pressed forward.

Then, a miraculous occurrence. I came to a line of policemen. They stood abreast, arms linked, facing the crowd. Behind them, runners were being cleared from the course to ease congestion. And just like that, I stood at the front of the mob, toeing the cobblestones like a racer at the starting line. Behind me were thousands of runners and a dozen bulls waiting to be released. Before me—and the dozen others standing alongside me up front—was nothing but the empty cobblestones of Mercaderes Street. Six hundred yards and several sharp turns out of sight was the bullfighting coliseum. As I stared ahead, unable to believe my good fortune, a street-cleaning truck rumbled down that corridor, sweeping up glass and hosing away puddles. To top it all off, Ron and the pilots suddenly appeared at my side. I was oh so glad to see them, for I was getting very nervous indeed. "Hey," Ron said. I could tell from the rapid way his eyes shifted and his rapid speech that he was getting nervous, too. "We thought we lost you."

Then the rockets went off back by the bulls' corral, signaling their release. The policemen, suddenly looking very afraid, dashed to the side of the street and pressed their bodies into a vestibule.

The run was on.

At first I sprinted just to avoid being trampled. Then, as we settled into a powerful pace and I found myself drafting on the tail end of a small lead pack, I reveled in how incredibly surreal it felt to be leading the charge during the running of the bulls. The cobblestones were slick from the street washer (television footage would later show a bull slipping and nearly crushing a half-dozen runners during the ninety-degree right turn from Mercaderes Street to Estafeta Street). I was careful with my footing as I rounded the turn. I stayed to the outside, lest I get pinned against the fence. I never looked over my shoulder, but I was always listening for the clatter of hooves. The average time it takes the bulls to go from their enclosure to the Plaza de Toros is three minutes and fifty-five seconds. Time had become fluid and compressed. But I knew they would be coming soon.

The charge up Estafeta Street was made tougher by a two-percent grade. Runners started falling back, me included. The weight had become an issue. No longer was I in the lead but ten yards behind the pack. I struggled to maintain contact, if only for the sheer thrill of running up front. At the top end of Estafeta, where it meets Bajada de Javier, barricades had been installed on both sides. Uniform-clad spectators hung sidesaddle on the horizontal slats like cowboys cheering a roundup. Just like in a roundup, the fences were narrowing into a funnel. The run was at its most dangerous in this *telefonica* as bulls and runners were compressed into the narrow passage. There would be no escaping an angry animal. I sprinted through, always listening for but still not hearing the thunder of hooves.

Then there it was: the Plaza de Toros. The finish. Some spectators dropped down off the barriers and ran those last hundred yards into the coliseum. This struck me as cheating—they had taken no risk but could forever claim to have run with the bulls. This area, known as the Callejon, was as far as Hemingway got.

It's ironic that Hemingway wrote the definitive text on running with the bulls yet missed the best part.

We raced single file down the Callejon, into the darkness of the stadium tunnel. I could see the dirt of the arena straight ahead. Patches were still stained crimson from where bulls had died the night before.

The moment we burst from the tunnel into the pastel sunlight of the bullfighting arena will stay with me forever. Thousands of Spaniards—a seamless carpet of red and white—were on their feet cheering and waving their arms. I recognized the roar. It was that splendid peal reserved for the very good matadors. Even though it wasn't directed at me alone, such sublime glory occurs infrequently in life, and it must be cherished. When I reached the center of that dusty ring, I stopped, then twirled slowly to take it all in. Ron made it a few seconds later. So did all the other pilots. We smacked each other on the back and captured the moment with Ron's pocket digicam.

Then the bull charged. An offshoot of the herd had come in right behind us. One singled me out. Just in time, I heard the hollow thunder of hooves and a subtle gasp from the crowd. I sprinted like a cowardly matador for the red arena wall. Vaulting the barricade, I landed atop two Pamplona policemen. They pummeled my hamstrings with billy clubs in the international gesture of benevolence, then threw me bodily from the coliseum.

Regardless, I was awash in grace, knowing something very special had just taken place. Encierro legend says that a runner surviving a close brush with a bull has been protected by the cloak of San Fermin. That's how I felt.

I wandered, riding an adrenaline high, to a café. There I sipped an espresso and read an American newspaper at a tin table adorned with a single red ashtray. It was the same plaza as the day before but now empty. And silent. I put the paper down and ordered another espresso, then sat for an hour, just thinking. Something had happened back there in the arena; something had changed.

It wasn't the cheers that made the time on the dirt floor so wondrous, I concluded: It was the participating. The pushing limits. It's one thing to write about the exploits of others, as I'd been doing for so long. It's quite another to get out there and do it myself.

It was a sensation so fulfilling, I wanted to make it a regular part of my life. Not as an occasional experience but on a daily basis. So as I sat there in the pale blue Pamplona dawn, wired on caffeine and adrenaline and the draped aura of San Fermín, I made a resolution: Every day for a year I would focus on pushing my limits. Being the best I could be. Not just in work but in all things. I didn't know if it was possible, but I figured it couldn't hurt to give it a try.

I had no idea what would happen during that year or what conclusions I might reach when it was over. I only knew that I had to step outside my comfort zone and push.

PAMPLONA (PART III)

"Married?"

"Yes."

"Kids?"

"Three boys."

"What are your goals?"

"My what?"

"Your goals. What do you want to be when you grow up?"

Oh. You mean quests.

It was a scorching Southern California morning. Smog draped over the sun-dried hills like a coffee-colored veil. The 91 and 405 were bumper to bumper because everyone from Riverside was on their way to the beach. I rode a stationary bike in the air-conditioned House of Pain, two weeks after running with the bulls. The optimism of that ponderous morning had survived the journey and led me to commit an act of minor humility: hiring a personal trainer. Like most men, I consider the sports and fitness universe my personal domain. Paying someone to tell me how to work out, like asking directions, was an admission of weakness. Trainers are for bloated, out-of-shape, over-the-hill, bearing-less men who lack the discipline to condition themselves properly. Even after realizing I had become just such a man, the decision to hire a trainer felt embarrassing—and surprisingly difficult.

I had seen scores of trainers at the gym over the years, leaning on the weight machines and chatting with their clients about their weekends. What struck me was that these trainers (many of whom looked like they could use a trainer themselves) had the same clients month after month, but rarely—if ever—did I see evidence of increased fitness or weight loss. What I was searching for was an individual whose fitness, knowledge, and presence I respected. Someone with a plan that would produce results. Someone, without putting too fine a point on it, who was more interested in kicking my ass than being my pal.

Terry Sedgewick was hulking and shiny bald, with the shaved legs and tree-trunk thighs of a professional bike racer and the maniacal snarl of an elite rugby player. He had given up both those pastimes to study exercise physiology and become a personal trainer. His clients ran the gamut from movie stars to housewives and high school cheerleaders to professional baseball players. And, beginning on that sweltering July morning, me.

Terry's windowless gym was in a no-nonsense concrete building across the street from a cement plant. It had no sign out front. Parking was atrocious. His clients, one and all, knew it as the House of Pain. I stepped inside for my first training session. The tang of dried sweat hung in the artificially cool air. Rust flecked the weights racked against unpainted walls, the oxidation produced by countless droplets of perspiration. Two beat-up treadmills and two direct-drive stationary bikes faced a video monitor playing a tape of the Tour de France with the audio turned down. Pastel medicine balls were scattered about the all-weather carpeting like enormous, spongy marbles awaiting a giant shooter. Clearly, the House of Pain was not a place to be seen or to make conversation. It was a place to work.

I was paying by the hour. The clock began the instant I set foot in the door. Terry interviewed me while I warmed up on a bike, trying to divine whether I was interested in fitness or merely losing weight.

The goal question stumped me for two reasons. First, I had no goals. I just wanted to be *better*. Second, the definitive answer was complex and went something like this: We all have quests. They are sometimes called adventures or odysseys or even, at their most pedestrian, goals. (I despise the term. It reminds me of my father's belief that his oldest son was becoming an aimless layabout because I had no "goals.") Quests are quixotic. They are life's great lubricant, easing the passage through the successive portals from birth to death. Quests are personal. They cannot be contrived. The path from conception to completion is random, interconnected, tangential, and whimsical; daring, desperate, hungry, and pure, as if God is unveiling an audacious plan and asking us to take a leap of faith and go along for the ride. Born in the soul, the offspring of a dream, and so unrealistic at the outset as to be ludicrous, quests nudge us from the complacency of everyday life into a realm of discomfort, struggle, and, if all goes according to plan, success. Either way, there's growth. And either way, soon after completion another quest beckons, quiet as a whisper.

My quests have been far ranging: to finish college, to convince a beautiful brown-eyed girl to marry me, to buy a house, to quit my corporate job and become a full-time writer, to finish the Raid Gauloises. To write the Africa book.

Each, against long odds, was realized.

The Pamplona resolution was not yet a quest. It was an admission that it was time to change how I went about my life. I had begun the journey without knowing where I wanted to go and without a map to show me the way. Seeing a personal trainer seemed the logical place to start. Asking where the journey would go next was a question I couldn't comprehend. "I'd like to lose some weight," I admitted to Terry, pulling an obvious result out of the air.

"Hop off the bike," he ordered, handing me a pair of dumbbells. They were pink and weighed two pounds each. "Jog in place and punch your arms straight up and down." It was not as simple as it looked. I began sweating as my heart rate shot up. "Now," he said with frightening intensity. His voice had that unnerving inflection of cinematic sociopaths, an inappropriate cheerfulness in the midst of my suffering. "You're probably wondering why you're using those little girlie weights."

I guess I was supposed to answer, but I couldn't.

"The reason is you've got way too much crap on your upper body. The last thing you need is more bulk." He held out his hand for the dumbbells, which now weighed fifty pounds apiece. "I'll take those. Okay now, run in place, kicking heels to butt as fast as you can. Go."

It was not personal training as I'd imagined. For the next

hour I barely touched another weight, but I sweated so much that it puddled in my shoes, making a squishing noise as I jumped, leapt, and ran in place; push-upped, lunged, squatted, and crunched. The abdominal exercises alone were so extensive and devious that the following morning, whenever I tried to take a deep breath, my torso spasmed as if baseball bats were hammering me from the inside out. I was, in a most unconventional way, getting my ass kicked.

"What do you want to get out of this?" he asked as the hour came to an end. I was light-headed and experiencing tunnel vision. "You were an athlete once. You're capable of more than just losing weight."

As always, it comes back to the writing. I remembered the Borders manager in Albuquerque. "I want to look good in my author photo," I blurted. An answer so honest it was embarrassing. Even though I had just read a magazine piece emphasizing the role an attractive author photo plays in selling books—and despite my fervent longing that the Africa book sell ten million copies, become a major motion picture, and give me a measure of financial peace after a decade of struggle—it sounded vain to say so out loud.

"We can make you a pretty boy," he answered. "That part's easy."

Terry paused to watch Lance Armstrong on the video monitor, standing in the pedals to attack. "Are you sure you don't want to do more?"

WEATHER OR NOT

Just last week I was in New York, where the temperature was below freezing and the raw windchill made it feel twenty degrees colder. I knew that if I stepped out of the hotel for a run, I'd be miserable for about three blocks, but by the time I got to Central Park I'd actually be sweating. I also knew that I had all the right gear for foul-weather running: gloves, stocking cap, tights, and a thick sweatshirt that would make me feel downright cozy. I knew that if I ran just twenty minutes, it would alter my mood for the better, buoying me the rest of the day. If I ran longer—maybe forty minutes or even an hour—I would know the stiff backbone of having overcome Mother Nature. Throughout the day I would think back to my run and feel that little burst of sunshine in my heart for overcoming my doubts.

But I didn't. I headed down to the hotel fitness center, where I got bored on the treadmill after just three minutes. A couple of pushups, a few situps, and all too soon I was back in my room polishing off a second cup of coffee while poring over *USA Today*.

And then came that inevitable moment of confrontation with my wimpiness. As I left the hotel for a meeting on Fifth

Avenue, I cut through the park. Not only was it a brisk but gorgeous day for running, with a layer of snow turning the landscape into someplace new and exciting, but it was packed with runners. Hats on their heads, gloves on their hands, those hardy souls were out in force.

That's the thing about weather. More than any other excuse, it seems a viable reason for not running. And if the run actually takes place, I'd put the odds at better than eighty percent that it's a survival run that feels more like obligation than the sort of uplifting workout that makes the rest of the day lighter.

Therein lies the question: When is the run an obligation instead of a joy? When are weather conditions truly prohibitive, and when are they a convenient excuse? It's one of the great inner debates in endurance sports, as my runners have learned. We all have a personal limit, a redline that we cross at our peril. Running two hours in one-hundred-degree heat is too much for me, but for a Hawaiian Ironman it's no big deal. To me, running in a blizzard is stupid, but I've done it. Running in the rain is uplifting or miserable, depending upon the size of the drops and the force of the wind. Warm rain on a tropical island is refreshing. A cold, driving rain on a January afternoon as the sun sets, five miles from home, is miserable.

And yet, if I am wearing a hat, running in that January rain can be fortifying. A hat keeps the rain out of my eyes and off my head and my core temperature elevated, preventing hypothermia. Somehow, even when my hands are numb and my chest soaked, having that little island of comfort atop my hair is quite nice indeed. One of my favorite running memories began during half-time of an NFL play-off game a few years back. I flipped off the TV and popped out for a couple of quick miles. The rain set in long after I'd stretched beyond two miles to something that would eventually become eight. At the furthest possible point from home, the sky turned black and the rain pounded down. But I had my hat. All seemed right with the world. The day felt just a little more epic for the rain and the wind, as if I was having some sort of Frozen Tundra play-off experience of my own. I jacked up the pace so I could make it home for the fourth quarter. When I remember that run, I think of stepping back in the house just as Brett Favre threw a touchdown pass. I think of cold, hard rain lashing my torso. I think of the baseball cap that kept my mood upbeat and my head toasty. And I think of the marvelously hot shower that turned my skin lobster-red as it restored circulation to my extremities.

I find it curious that people who live in California run on treadmills inside climate-controlled gyms far more than people back east. When I am in London, I often marvel at the sheer number of runners chugging through Hyde Park, no matter the conditions. These people inspire me and make me question my motivation when I am wont to take the day off on account of weather. When I was in New York last week, for instance, it's not like I spent that blustery day cooped up inside my hotel. No. There was work to be done. I walked across town, walked back, went out to dinner. In fact, I walked back to my hotel in a freezing rain. So why couldn't I have endured that same weather for the sake of the run? Simple: I used the weather as an excuse.

It goes back to my premise about why we run in the first place. The act of running is a decision to be the best possible version of ourselves. It is a striving to be more than mediocre, if only for that burst of time we're out there getting it done. Most days the act of stepping outside the door is made more difficult by worry, bills, time constraints, and other everyday issues of life. So to make that decision even more difficult by adding weather as an obstacle seems almost unfair. But the choice to run despite the weather is fortifying. I think about the faces of the Hyde Park runners and how they seemed so unafraid. You don't earn that look by taking the day off on account of weather. At the risk of offending gym rats everywhere, I also don't think you get that look on a treadmill.

I should add that the denizens of Hyde Park don't look crazy. That's the look of people who run in blizzards and lightning storms and at noon in the desert, where the run borders on obligation or obsession. The season when I worked on *Survivor,* my favorite run on the island was along the beach, where the sand was white and the South China Sea was the most inspiring shade of blue-green. But the instant one of those tropical storms hit, with those BBs of rain shooting down from the sky and the thunder exploding so close it felt like it was inside my skull, I would have been a madman to venture onto that beach. What would be the point?

I want to know that line between strong and crazy. To not go outside when wildfire has fouled the air. To never be more than a few hundred yards from the water trolley when the mercury spikes.

And to always wear a hat in the rain.

PAMPLONA (PART IV)

More?

Once upon a time I'd posed that same question to myself, but I'd phrased it differently. It was soon after finishing the nine years of bacchanal I like to refer to as "college," on my first day working for a large corporation. All my life I'd believed in the ideal that there was a certain progression to success and to life itself: elementary school, junior high school, high school, college, career, marriage, children, retirement, death. Happiness, fulfillment, and a comfortable sense of wealth were by-products of this linear continuum. Central to it all was the concept of career, and that's where I got stuck.

Not in the career itself, but in deciding the profession to which I would devote my life. The only two things I was passionate about were running and writing. Running was a competitive pastime and a source of deep personal fulfillment but not a lifelong career. Writing, as my mother informed me at the age of six, wasn't much better. "Nobody makes a living as a writer," she scolded me sternly when I told her of my ambition to write books. That nugget of truth firmly planted in my brain, I labored through those long years of college, trying to think of something else for which I was suited. Until I divined the perfect career, graduating seemed pointless. How could I move on to Marriage and Children if I didn't have a Career about which I was deeply passionate? My father was a pilot, and one of my most vivid childhood memories was him drinking beer and barbecuing in the backyard, joking and boasting as he talked flying with his fellow pilots. They spoke with their hands, putting their beers down and having the flattened left palm chase the right, demonstrating some maneuver they'd performed in the sky that day, already eager to be up in the air again first thing in the morning. Later, when I paid my college bills by bartending, I mentally compared memories of those enthusiastic faces with those of the beaten men and women who took a stool each afternoon, bitching about their jobs and living for the weekend. I didn't know what I wanted to do with my life, but I knew I didn't want to be like them.

It took me so long to finish college that my mother suggested I give up and join the circus—not Ringling Brothers but the off-brand little circus that visited El Toro Marine Base every year. I don't know which was worse: my mother's certainty that the best I could hope for was a lifetime of mucking elephant excrement, perhaps someday to marry a limber Hungarian trapeze artist (or maybe just have a common-law arrangement with some toothless carnie possessing a fondness for screw-top wine and homemade speed), or, just as startling, that I actually entertained the notion.

What stopped me was the certain knowledge that even if I escaped into that world for a year or ten, the failure to finish college would nag at me. I would be forced to return and get a degree, because college was the next step to where I wanted to go, even though I didn't know where I was going.

All that changed when I met Calene, a graduate student at USC with whom I fell deeply in love. We made plans to marry. Suddenly, it didn't matter what kind of degree I had—just that I had one. Three months after the wedding—and three months and two days after I graduated—I reported for my first day at my brand-new corporate job. I wore a suit and tie, carried an empty briefcase, and tried my very best to look excited about my new career in procurement. I expected a world of ambitious men and women who would engage me daily in philosophical debate. There would be travel. I would parlay my middling starting salary into something six-figure-ish.

The workday started at 7 a.m. By noon, rattled by the knowledge that it didn't take a college intellect to perform the data entry that had occupied my morning and that my career path was veering toward the dangerously meaningless, there was just one question on my mind: Is this as good as it gets?

In the days to come I learned two important things. First, that nobody I ever met in the corporate world knew what they wanted to do with their life. Where they lived, how they lived, and what sort of work they did was for the corporation to tell them.

And second, I had to get out.

The quest to do more with my life began then. So when Terry asked the question fifteen years later, it was nothing new.

After putting the final touches on *Into Africa,* with its all-consuming writing and research process, I was so wrung out that I felt incapable of writing a single sentence, let alone a next book. The Pamplona quest was the figurative deep breath I needed before embarking on a new leg of life's journey; a ritual purification, an emotional detox. I needed a break, and now Terry was asking if I were capable of more. Not bloody likely.

But then I had a thought.

Before I go into that thought, I should point out that few people realize they are entertaining outlandish notions that will seem, in retrospect, to be the sure sign of a midlife crisis. At the time, it just seems like a good idea. A very good idea—the fulfillment of some long-cherished dream and the making of one's self.

So that night, sipping Chardonnay out on the deck with Calene, watching the summer sun slip from the sky, I quietly vowed to put all the years of knowledge, my thousands of miles of training, and the interwoven strands of genetic fusion that composed my running life into a brand-new adjunct to my writing career.

That's right: I was going to get myself back in shape and try out for the U.S. Olympic team.

Nope. No midlife crisis there.

TOUGH GUY

What I desperately need right now are the simple things: ibuprofen, a hot shower, a large box of Q-tips. Antibiotics, thanks to the sheer tonnage of pasture effluent that invaded what the ancient Egyptians called "the seven openings of the head," will be vital. But these must wait until I fly home, as must the cleansing of my foul racing gear. My shorts, shirt, and socks are currently limning a permanent oval of mud around the heretofore virgin white bathroom sink in Wolverhampton's Ely House Hotel. My running shoes, meanwhile, will be left behind when I check out in the morning, too emotionally scarred to ever run an honest mile again. As if all that weren't enough, a glance into the mirror shows a man with a face lined and gray, at least two decades older than his actual age.

I look, quite frankly, broken.

Thus is my life after Tough Guy, a seven-mile odyssey of pain, suffering, and frozen water immersion. The title is tongue-in-cheek, but the cruel severity of the competition is not. Since its inception in 1994, Tough Guy has become an increasingly worldwide phenomenon, beckoning otherwise sane men and women to the

British Midlands in the dead of winter, there to sprint through pastures, scramble through thorns, jitterbug through electric cattle prods dangling like Portuguese man-of-war from ropes strung above knee-deep mud, climb and descend acres of cargo netting, and swim underwater through an icy pond.

There is icy and there is *icy*, so let me explain the concept of Tough Guy icy in order that you might better understand what happens here: During the 2006 race, competitors actually had to break through frozen pond ice for the privilege of full-body submersion. Seven hundred competitors later broke down from hypothermia, while more than a dozen were so numb that they simply toppled off the large obstacles and broke some sort of bone. Folks like me—and many of you—saw this as a litmus test. Tough Guy applications almost doubled the next year.

This is the terminus of the running boom, and it is something far beyond the passive metronome of the Hawaiian Ironman, where competitors pound out their miles in quiet, monotonous hell. Tough Guy, with its bagpipes and mud and frozen Borats, is a massive mutation of competition into something primal and potentially deadly.

It's as if endurance racing has not moved toward something more modern and sleek and welcoming for the sheer act of being simpler, but backward—*to toughness;* to a time and place when mankind raced through mud and cold because rapid forward locomotion was the only sort of feral behavior that kept him alive.

They line us up just before "eleven-ish," standing on the brow of a hill as strange men dressed like pirates weed out the poseurs who have dared move forward and infiltrate the Front Squad. I wear a trash bag with holes poked out for my head and arms, draped over my running kit to keep out the freezing chill until the starting gun, even as my hardier British compatriots wear just shorts and a T-shirt. There is great hilarity in watching the pretenders evicted: Their race bibs are a different color and bear monikers of increasing insult—Wetnecks, Late Comers, Dickheads.

As the select few of us constituting the Front Squad await the inevitable cannon blast that will launch us into Tough Guy, Mr. Mouse places the offenders into nearby stocks, where they are roundly jeered by the thousands of spectators and racers. Somewhere on the hillock behind us, bagpipers begin some sort of patriotic dirge. Mr. Mouse, a stoic man with a gray walrus mustache and mysterious past, steps to one side of the long frozen line of Front Squad. Now seems a good time to strip off the trash bag and feel the brisk winter air against my skin.

Just then, at eleven-ish on the dot, Tough Guy begins.

If it sounds horrible, it is. And yet . . .

If you can imagine an endurance race that combines the absurd best of Monty Python with the punishing numbness of Navy SEAL training, then you can comprehend Tough Guy. Going one step further: If you are the sort of person who cannot just imagine such a race but also hears an irrational voice in the back of your brain as you read this essay (something you randomly plucked off a shelf in the bookstore but now wonder if it was some act of fate), curious if you are, indeed, Tough Enough, then I am almost positive that some January very soon, no matter the status of your marriage or career or credit card balances, you will not consider your life complete until a Tough Guy finisher medal hangs around your neck.

You know who you are.

My story: I first learned of Tough Guy on a flight from Hong Kong to Los Angeles years back, watching race footage on a small seat-back screen. My headphones didn't work, and I was half asleep. Yet those miserable images of filthy, drenched bodies that made the competitors resemble Agincourt reenactors called out to me. It was a kindred spirit of sorts, and I knew I had to be part of it. I did not find Tough Guy, as it were. Tough Guy found me.

A sulphureous chum of yellow smoke envelops the Front Squad as we gallop down the first quarter-mile of pasture, knowing that the rest of the pack will soon be racing to catch up. Eyes burn. Throats sting. My feet search for smooth purchase, knowing all too well that a simple buckle in the turf can roll an ankle and make my race even more daunting before it actually kicks into high gear. I suppose I could quit if I broke an ankle. Anybody could.

But what sort of man flies a fourth of the way around the world, leaving behind wife and children to validate his Tough Guy-ness, only to come up short within the opening minutes? I've been there, my friends. I've been there. I raced a mountain bike through the jungles of Saipan on a bare rim rather than face my wife's inevitable look of disappointment after dropping out because of two flat tires 5,000 miles from home. Sometimes being a Tough Guy just means holding up your end of the spousal compact. Know what I mean?

The first course of mud comes soon after, a simple dirt road turned filthy by rain and too many footfalls. My body is now spattered with flecks of cold mud. I feel warm because I am running hard, and I wonder how long this sense of comfort will last. We churn a mile through a pasture, and the pack settles into a rhythm. This is just like any other Sunday run so far—that is, until we start scrambling through the nettles.

Tough Guy is held the last Sunday in January, outside rural Wolverhampton. This former hub of the Industrial Revolution is now known for wine shops and small country estates. (Just so you know, there is also a summer Tough Guy, but as one competitor wondered aloud at the starting line, "What's the point?" Meaning no self-respecting Tough Guy prefers to race there when it's warm. With which I wholeheartedly agree.)

Approaching the course on race day, one sees nothing but bucolic green countryside populated here and there by sheep. Suddenly, great log towers rise sixty feet into the sky like some holdover from a Roman siege. Cargo nets and flags of all nations cling to the towers, somewhat absurdly. And then you drive a little further and come upon a mass of half-dressed humanity who paid unfathomable money to clamber up and down these nets.

How much? I shelled out $400 *extra* for the privilege of starting in the Front Squad, rather than getting stuck behind the great mass of humanity further back. (It's worth noting that I didn't even bother asking my accountant if I could write it off as a business expense, knowing that such an ungodly figure would be dismissed as some weird sort of fantasy by the IRS. Look, you pay the money out of passion. No other way to explain it.)

There is a low crawl after the nettles, followed by a clamber over a hay bale, a pattern that is repeated for the next mile. My body heat begins to dissipate as the course forces us to leap into a shallow stream, cross the knee-deep water to the other bank, clamber up and out onto the pasture, and then repeat the process countless times. Soon after, the race gets hard: the cargo netting, the tire tunnels, the flaming bales of hay.

And all the while the mud gets more frequent and the water crossings get deeper, until my feet are numb and it has become commonplace to wade through water up to my chest. I think the worst has come.

I am wrong.

I read back my words just now, looking for some form and structure. There is none. These are the ramblings of a man whose brain has been frozen by sharp spikes of cold water and who has only recently seen the Seinfeldian concept of cold water shrinkage no longer having such an obvious effect on his lower extremities. (The water was so cold—and I can say this because we are all friends by now—that I could actually feel my lower appendages scrambling, turtlelike, to recede inside the relative warmth of my torso. No lie.)

How is it possible to suffer so completely and have such a great time? I'm still not sure. All I know is that I have scratches and scrapes up and down my body and the remains of a Sharpie'd race number still beaming indelibly from my forehead. Tough Guy logic stipulates that body marking anywhere else makes no sense.

What is it like to leap into a freezing lake in January, not once but several times, and hold your breath and swim underwater—all of this after miles of running, cargo nets, and electric shock? Let's just say that the race organizers are clever gentlemen. They throw the first instance of midrace baptism at the competitors at that exact point when the numbing reality of incredible hardship has worn off and the brain has just begun to cope like a Tough Guy muscle all its own, uttering such thoughts as "This isn't so bad" and "I think the worst is behind me."

Which, as you all know, is one of those lies we all tell ourselves when life gets tough.

Tough Guy gets incrementally harder, mile by mile, and hides its difficulties by having the course weave around on itself. I never know what's coming next, and also never know how long that particular challenge will be repeated (the endless succession of low crawls followed by stream wading was particularly cruel, softening us all up for the fiery pits and then the first cargo net climb to the top of a tall tower, which was immediately followed by a high elevation rope crossing). Mr. Mouse gamely reminded all competitors that he does not have insurance. If I slip and break something (large signs point to the room where plaster casts are applied), it's "my own damned fault," as the race waiver says.

The race took me 1:35 to finish, and most folks seem to get done within an hour or so of that. Seven thousand people competed today. There were women, men, SAS soldiers, and Navy SEALs; two guys with "Air Force Academy Rugby" gear bags who painted their bodies red, white, and blue; and a guy who raced in a Day-Glo green Borat-style banana hammock. The first few miles you just flat-out race, but after that, there's a shared solidarity. Having trouble getting over a wall? Some friendly hand will shove you up and over. Wondering when your feet will stop being numb? Someone whose feet are clearly just as numb will run alongside, coated head to toe in mud, reminding you that no one is immune from the challenges. The best days in life are like that, too.

There is a moment in the last mile when I've already gone into the icy waters one too many times and climbed what I thought was my last high-altitude cargo net and can see that the next obstacle is to walk a plank off the side of a tower and take a twenty-foot plunge into yet more icy water, immediately followed by a thirty-meter swim to shore. It is a moment when my body screams that it will not be able to withstand another bout of immersion. Men and women are just behind, breathless and shivering, waiting their turn to walk the plank—just so we can all get this silly race over with.

I have been frozen and filthy for too long. I do not care if I am tough or not. I cannot stand the thought that I must, inevitably, jump. This is not a race moment of exhilaration or pride but a midrace "I am broken" moment. Hypothermia has set in. I do not know how I will pull this off.

A guy next to me mumbles to himself "Get it done" as he eyes the drop. But it is as though he is talking to me, for I know exactly how he feels.

There is some sort of perverse personal growth that takes place when you ignore the fearful voice telling you not to leap. It is that moment when you simply take a bold step forward and fling yourself off the plank, knowing that the next sensation of cold and immersion will suck very, very, very much. I can't describe why pushing through those self-doubts and fears of being uncomfortable makes me feel so damned happy, but it does. It's why I do these races again and again, just to confront that voice and do battle with myself to see whether or not, on that given day, ambition or fear will win out.

So I leapt. The freefall was short and the seconds underwater far too long. I sputtered to the surface, swam to shore, and then flung myself down into the mud to low crawl beneath barbed wire as part of an obstacle named for the Battle of the Somme. There was much more hardship to come (yes, more icy water), but finally crossing that finish line and sipping my cup of hot tea with shaking hypothermic hands was a most amazing moment of happiness.

I honestly don't believe you can know that feeling without some great personal challenge, whether it's Mr. Mouse's footrace or any other of life's adventures. As the man on the plank said in that moment of reckoning, being a Tough Guy is about finding a way to get it done.

All right. That's as profound as I get in this reduced state. Now, if you'll excuse me, I'm long overdue for that hot shower.

PAMPLONA (PART V)

London is bitter cold as I slip out of the Connaught for a run. It is 5 a.m., but it feels like midnight because the winter sky is so absolutely dark. I walk the first block, still half asleep, eating a crisp red apple plucked from a bowl in the lobby, debating whether or not a run is really necessary. I have no set route in mind, no set distance. The ambitious part of me wants to get in a few miles; the more reasonable half thinks that rising from bed was accomplishment enough. Proceeding further than the corner would be excessive.

I compromise, reminding myself of my Olympic goal, knowing that I am trying to trick myself into a solid workout. The plan, I tell myself, is to jog slowly around Grosvenor Square, then back to the room. Total distance: a half-mile, maybe less. Definitely less. Which is okay. No sense catching a cold. Work up a good sweat, do abs on the hotel carpet, drink a lot of water before finding succor in that first cup of coffee, then hit that Russian place for eggs Florentine the instant they open. I put the apple core in a rubbish bin and begin trotting down Carlos Place, feeling stiff in my back and hamstrings and noncommittal from head to toe.

All I want is an easy trot before a day of research. It's easier to get it out of the way now than to fit it in later—in which scenario I'd leave the library, take the Underground back to the hotel, change into running clothes, run, shower, then return to the library. I'd never make it back. Somewhere between the run and the shower, I'd find it a whole lot more inviting to grab a book and head to the Red Lion for a pint. Running early keeps me honest.

Whoa. Need to pay attention. A cab—the only car on the road, so you'd think I'd see it straightaway—almost creams me as I step off the curb in front of the Indonesian embassy. The city of London has painted signs on the ground at every intersection, reminding pedestrians which way to look for oncoming traffic. "Look Right." "Look Left." A helpful arrow shows the way if you don't read English. Those signs have probably saved my life a dozen times. This morning is another. Maybe one of these days I won't have to be told which way to look. In the meantime, I'm glad for the reminder. And suddenly very wide awake.

I glance to my left, toward the far end of the square. A pair of bobbies, automatic weapons dangling from their chests, guards the American embassy. I wince every time I see that hulking gray colossus. Boxy, ringed by chain-link fence, it looks like a penitentiary for bureaucrats. Two city blocks of tasteful Georgian homes must have been leveled to make way for the thing. It's appalling. No matter how many times I look at it, I can't find a sliver of appeal or character.

An early morning rant—a fine way to focus the mind. I trot on. My body is still on Southern California time. Morning feels like bedtime. I am tempted yet again to turn back. The wind is too cutting and the streets too desolate for a reasonable person to be running.

But I am not a reasonable person.

The wind is really howling as I turn onto broad, neon-lit Oxford Street. ("Great Shopping!" remarks my London map.) It stings my cheeks and numbs my gloveless hands. My legs are protected by tights and my torso by a thin fleece, but the wind goes through those, too. These are crappy conditions for a runner.

The feeling is heightened by the emptiness of the streets. I am alone. No early morning exercisers. No pedestrians. I pick up my pace as I run past the empty businesses: Gap, McDonald's, Bureau de Change. At Regent Street I feel like turning right, which will eventually take me to Piccadilly Circus. From there it's just a mile or so back to the hotel. I figure it'll be a three-mile workout, all told.

An adventurous thought enters my brain: I always turn right, so today turn left? Regent Street is not as bright or straight as Oxford Place, where I could see a mile into the distance. The Langham Hotel looms a half-mile up, where the road bends left. It was once the finest hotel in London. Mark Twain stayed there. Henry Morton Stanley did, too, even when he couldn't afford it. I chuckle even as I run, because I am like Stanley in that way. There's nothing so foreign about a foreign city that a great hotel can't cure.

Past the BBC building. Then the Kenyan embassy, which makes me self-conscious about my stride. It's as if the consular officials of that nation of great runners are casting a critical eye on my gait. A foolish thought, but, because proper stride is everything to a runner, I make sure my head is up and my pelvis thrust forward—"like at the point of deepest penetration," as legendary coach Bill Bowerman is said to have described optimal form.

I keep waiting for the sun to rise or at least wedge a blue sliver onto the horizon to show that it's preparing to make its entrance. But the sun does not rise, and I remember that London is at a high northern latitude. How far north, I don't know. As I arrive at Regent's Park, its sprawling green acreage now the dark and forbidding domain of muggers and anyone else waiting for a stupid person to run past in the darkness, I'm consumed in mental geography.

And, to my surprise, running rather quickly. The wind has stilled. I race along the ring road, footfalls echoing on the pavement. I have lost forty pounds since Pamplona. Changed my diet (less Snickers and Bass Ale; more protein and antioxidant-rich blueberries). Changed my work schedule so that I spend the first part of each morning hanging out with Calene. Changed my life to such a degree that I feel stronger, sharper, and more alive than at any time in memory. One constant has been running, the God-given talent that has buoyed me since childhood. The slow plod of the summer has been replaced by a more natural stride as the pounds went wherever it is pounds go.

But my pace this morning is altogether different, a kind of speed I knew back when I raced. My run feels effortless. So I go faster. On a whim, I make a sharp right turn into Regent's Park. The grass is saturated from heavy rain. Mud puddles have spilled over onto some of the trails, but all in all, Regent's Park is a fine place to run in the dark. Not a mass murderer in sight.

Another runner bursts out of the darkness. I inhale a frightened whoosh of air and stop abruptly, as if for a rattler. But the runner is already gone. I sprint madly down the path, sure I'm being chased. When the adrenaline subsides, I feel foolish for putting myself at risk. I rediscover my proper cadence and, with it, a sort of idiotic defiance. Now that I know that the locals do the same on a regular basis, I don't feel so crazy for running through the park in pitch black.

I charge back down Portland Place toward Regent Street. Or at least I think it's Portland Place. I am lost in the side streets of London, trying to find my way back to Mayfair. The narrow roads are becoming jammed with cars. I am constantly looking the wrong way when I cross. I think I find my way, only to realize I am back at Regent's Park. Forcing myself to be patient, I follow the flow of traffic, thinking this will get me back to the main streets. It works. Soon I am on Oxford Street again—there's the Gap, there's the McDonald's—and headed back toward the Connaught. It is still very cold and dark. There are runners everywhere along this broad boulevard, as well as commuters walking briskly up and down the gray sidewalks. Awash in the endorphin high of a great run and emboldened by the company, I stride past Duke Street, the turn for the hotel, and aim for Hyde Park.

I know it well. I race past the temporary ice rink and follow the bridle trails in their grand loop around the perimeter, then leave the trails and follow the unmowed contours of the inner park. The rolling hills are a challenging change of scenery after the flat streets and riding trails. A detour toward the Serpentine for a run past the

Peter Pan statue, then I sprint across the grass to the Speke obelisk, where I make it a point to pay tribute every time I run the park.

Speke, the exploration savant, another character from the Africa book. I come to a full stop at the monument, chiseled from red Aberdeen granite. Then I step over the black wrought-iron fence ringing the perimeter. I trace my hand across the plaque announcing that Speke discovered the source of the Nile. He didn't, though he came close. His accomplishments and bravery were spectacular nonetheless.

I am running again, finally ready to call it quits. It's hard to say how long I've been out, but London is wide awake. The sun is still hiding, but everyone is getting on with their day. And so must I.

Past the Albert Memorial. Past the Royal Geographical Society. Down the deep sand of Rotten Row, the riding trail that got its name back when it was a royal carriage path.

I cross under Park Lane through the pedestrian tunnel and start jogging once I reach the Audley Pub. The wind freezes the sweat on my head and down my back as I slow to a walk. It has been a very good run. Ten miles. Maybe more. I'm curious about where the speed came from, and I wonder, for the first time, how fast I am capable of going.

I had doubts about my Olympic quest, but no more. I am a runner again.

SAIPAN

The sweep vehicle was waiting as I hobbled from the jungle. The finish, after four hours of swimming, mountain biking, and running, was just a mile down a thin coral road. I was shaky from dehydration. A sweat of great salinity stung my eyes and pooled in my running shoes. My injured foot throbbed. I made the left turn toward the Pacific but could not yet feel its breeze. The driver raised his seat to the full upright position and turned the key, then followed at an impatient distance, as if last place was leprous.

That didn't bother me. I'd come to terms with last place hours ago—or so I told myself. What broke my heart was that my quixotic Olympic quest had come to an end. Even on runs like that bitter cold morning in London, my pace was dawdling by Olympic standards. It was time to let it go. The quest would end, not in Athens before a crowd of thousands, but on the tropical island of Saipan, bringing up the rear at the infamous XTERRA off-road triathlon, before one heavy-lidded broom truck driver.

A journey isn't an adventure until something goes wrong. My day at the Saipan XTERRA had been a most profound adventure, indeed.

The beginning of the end of the quest, which made up act one of the adventure, began one fine Saturday morning a few weeks earlier, right after a long training run. I was umpiring behind the plate at a Little League game when the redheaded kid on the mound threw a curveball that dropped below the catcher's glove.

Big league umps wear steel-toed shoes for just this reason. I wore my beloved Gel-Kayanos. That curveball landed on my big toe with astounding force and velocity, considering the pitcher was all of ten years old. A crimson stain spread over the front of my right running shoe as the nail split in two. Not wanting to look like a baby—it was, after all, just a toe wound—I kept umpiring.

An injury always leads to another injury. Before I knew it, I couldn't run for a week because the injured toe had become an injured calf, which made for a pained and hobbled stride. Which is when *Sports Illustrated* called to ask if I'd like to fly to Saipan and cover the XTERRA trail race. Of course I said yes. How else would I solve serious stride issues but by entering a race involving a one-mile swim, a fifteen-mile mountain bike, and a 7.4-mile trail run? Never mind that I hadn't swum a lap in five years. Or that my stride resembled the anguished shuffle of a man with IBS hotfooting it to the lavatory.

In reality, I already knew the quest was through. I was just too stubborn to let it go. That's why I accepted the assignment. Nothing,

I have learned, beats a great adventure for shedding perspective. XTERRA would be just what I needed.

XTERRA asks competitors to push their physical redline on courses notorious for difficulty—and ingenuity. The Saipan course, for instance, is an interactive tour of a World War II battlefield. On June 14, 1944, the veteran United States Marine Corps Second and Fourth Divisions, supported by the Army's Twenty-Seventh Division, invaded Saipan, the largest of the fourteen strategic Marianas Islands. The three-week battle was ferocious. In addition to the 3,000 American dead and more than 20,000 Japanese fatalities, thousands of Saipan natives flung themselves off cliffs, fearful that the Americans would eat them alive. Capturing Saipan, just 1,500 miles from Tokyo, meant American bombers were within range of Japan—indeed, the *Enola Gay* took off from Tinian, Saipan's sister island.

The XTERRA starting line was on the same beaches where Marines stormed ashore, then the course wound past Japanese pillboxes and into the jungle, through the same caves where Japanese forces hid during daylight. Rusting tanks, ordnance, and staff cars lined the course. War and adventure are unspoken bedfellows, but the two have never intertwined in such obvious fashion.

The water was the color of a robin's egg. Locals told me it was normally placid, but a cyclone to the west had breakers crashing onto the beach. The 150 competitors—an ironic contingent of Americans, Japanese, and Saipanese—splashed into the surf at the boom of the starter's cannon. The air was warm and tropical, and the gray marine layer was being parted by the sun. A strategy formed as I battled the currents and waves, my competitive juices kicking in: Muddle through the swim, pick competitors off with a solid bike leg, then grit my teeth and go for broke on the run, even if it meant doing more damage to my foot. If the Olympic quest was going to end, it was going down in a blaze of glory.

Glory. Such a conspicuous word. Can you find it standing in a bullring before a roaring crowd? In war? At the Olympics? And what strange tic in my genetic fiber makes glory an imperative? What's wrong with just pushing personal limits each and every day, not caring if anyone notices?

Over the next four hours, these thoughts spun in a continuous loop in my head. I finished the swim in a time too slow to mention, per strategy. But two miles into the cycling leg, my back tire went flat. I fixed it with my lone spare. A hundred yards later, the spare went flat. All of this took place in thick, muddy jungle, on narrow trails rippling with exposed roots and chunks of coral. The temperature was near one hundred. The humidity wasn't far behind. I stripped off the tire and began riding on the bare metal rim. It made a loud clanking noise on the coral and left a curious cleft in the mud, but at least I was still in the race.

The other competitors were soon miles ahead. At first it felt glorious muddling through such jungle on tempered steel (what a story I could tell!). Then adventurous. Then a reminder to persevere. Then it just sucked.

With every turn of the cranks, I lived the entire Kubler-Ross grieving process. I crashed. I ran out of water. I sunburned. The cleats on my bike shoes got stuck in my pedals, so that every time I crashed, I flopped over like a circus seal, still attached to the bike. When I wanted to push my broken rig through dank puddles or up slick hillsides, I had to intentionally crash first, then slip my feet from the shoes and traipse through the jungle muck in my socks. Lance Armstrong has never known this dark side of cycling.

I had plenty of time and solitude to think. So, among random ruminations that included Christopher Columbus, Bruce Springsteen, and my hotel room's tepid air-conditioning, I pondered the true nature of glory. More than once I thought of how silly my misadventures were in comparison to what the men who fought and died in that same jungle had gone through. Their personal quests died with them. From my prerace study of Saipan's American Memorial, I saw that most of the casualties were corporals and privates—teenagers who would never know the luxury of a midlife crisis.

So it was fitting that my quest ended as I pushed the bike to the top of Mount Tapotchau, site of some of the Saipan invasion's heaviest fighting. The quest had become an achievement-oriented fixation, I realized, not the complement to daily life it was meant to be. It slipped away without warning, like youth. My foot ached with each painful step. Perhaps it was reality setting in again.

So what had I gained? Well, without the quest I wouldn't have known Saipan's epiphanies. It wasn't the glory that made life wondrous, I remembered in my long hours in the tall jungle grass. It was the taking part. The pushing limits. Maybe I chased the quest just to realize that thought from Pamplona all over again.

What had been the point of my Olympic dream, that vainglorious and ultimately foolish chase that everyone but me saw as a shining emblem of midlife crisis? For starters, I was reminded of how much I loved running. When my oldest son began high school that fall, I'd watch the cross-country team while he was at football practice, remembering what it felt like to be so effortlessly fast—and longing to share the dozens of little tricks I'd learned over the years about how to run faster.

And then, of course, when Devin changed schools, I got a team all my own. None of that happens without Pamplona, without the House of Pain, without London and Saipan, and without the ultimate realization that my childhood dreams were done. It was time to grow up and dream again, this time as a man. No one was more surprised than me to find that these new dreams involved stepping outside myself to help others and, in the process, knowing a satisfaction and fulfillment I'd never imagined.

Encierro legend says that a runner surviving a close brush with a bull has been protected by the cloak of San Fermin. I think San Fermin spared me so I could foster the dreams of others, passing along the stuff I've learned over the years while also striving to rise above my own mediocrity through study and the daily discipline of coaching. My runners and I push each other to be ever better versions of ourselves. Which is why, every day I am out there, standing at every runner's spiritual home calling out splits, I feel as if I am awash in grace. "Those who bring sunshine into the lives of others, cannot keep it from themselves" is how *Peter Pan* author James M. Barrie described that feeling.

Bringing the sunshine isn't easy. Cross-country practice can be as frustrating and painful as that plunging curveball. My tone of voice can rise far above warm and fuzzy. I demand absurd levels of performance on absurd terrain in absurd weather conditions. I am mentor, despot, friend, motivator, teacher, water boy, timekeeper, judge, and jury. "Coaching," said former Stanford coach Brooks Johnson, "is no different from what a choreographer does with a dance or what a playwright does with a play."

I cherish that quote. It gives me purpose as I coalesce the creativity of writing with the discipline of coaching, and I am again reminded that success is not achieved in the comfort zone.

I know that lesson well. My job is to pass it on.

THE GOOD FIGHT

The run was frustrating and surprisingly dull. I was in northern Italy's Dolomite Mountains, on the shores of Lake Garda. It is a tourist destination. The waterfront boulevards were filled with travelers from around the world, sipping latte in the cafés, piloting rented Vespas, and piling out of their great diesel tour buses. A half-mile inland, pavement gave way to small farms and vineyards, and then to the towering forest-covered hills ringing the lake. One in particular featured a thousand-foot cliff rising straight up from the lakefront highway.

The shoreline was pretty and the town was a postcard, but I wanted to run through those forests. Yet after a full hour of searching for a trail, I'd found nothing. Every newfound wilderness path led into some farmer's backyard and the potential for a possibly awkward conversation about respecting property rights. Just as I was about to give up, I spied a little weathered nothing of a sign and an arrow pointing mysteriously to something called the Madonna d'Pigns.

I visualized a statue, a grotto, a haven in the woods where I might drop to one knee and loft a quiet prayer before turning back.

Following the arrow, I began climbing a short flight of steps between two ancient stone houses. The path had a rustic and unmanicured look. The town gave way to forest. I chugged upward. The steps were steeper than they looked. My quads began to burn. Fifty yards later, at what I thought was the top, there was no sign of any Madonna, only a path hooking sharply to the left and further upward into the forest. I kept on climbing. The forest was empty and still. There were no houses, no animals that I could see, no cars or mountain bikes. Just those endlessly upward stone steps and me.

The path kept getting steeper and steeper until the uphill produced the sort of midrun meditation where the mind wanders to some amazing and unlikely places. First I got to thinking about a call I'd gotten from an editor friend named Luke Smith. He'd just moved back to Alaska and had too much time on his hands, so I sent him some of these essays. His most pointed critique took me by surprise: "I can't believe you really thought you were going to make the Olympic team."

The comment nagged at me. Six years had passed since the quest. I'd never once doubted my motivations. But his words had gotten me to thinking.

The truth? I woke each and every day with the conviction that I would make the Olympic team. I had to. Empowered by that dream in my heart, I slipped on my shoes, and jetted out the door for the first of my two daily runs, feeling myself getting faster and more powerful with each and every footfall. Hope kept me going. More than that, it made my far-fetched dream seem quite rational— and attainable.

I climbed. Still no Madonna. I was beginning to doubt she existed. Mr. Keep Pushing . . . Always was quite done with pushing, climbing, and anything to do with the Madonna. I decided to turn around. But just then, a husband and wife became visible in the distance above me, hiking up the trail with great determination. Now I had no choice but to press on. If I went back to my hotel without finding the Madonna, it would be an admission that these hikers were made of sturdier stuff.

Damning my petty insecurities, I pressed on. Again, step by step, my mind wandered. Luke was replaced by aphorisms. To be a runner is to know aphorisms. An entire T-shirt and bumper sticker industry is devoted to supplying runners with some bold or witty statement that defines their outlook: *Runners Keep It Up Longer; Trample the Weak and Hurdle the Dead; Half-Marathons: They're Short, and I Like It Like That;* and on and on. The great Steve Prefontaine is featured on so many shirts that he's an aphorism profit center unto himself: *I don't race to win, I race to see who has the most guts; To give anything less than your best is to sacrifice the gift;* and my personal favorite, *What I want is to be number one.*

Great stuff. Powerful stuff. And sometimes those are exactly the sorts of words I need to get out of bed in the morning and put in my miles.

Which got me thinking about *Keep pushing . . . always.*

I never set out to coin an aphorism. Used improperly, aphorisms define trite. So why in the world did I come up with those three words that now conclude each e-mail to my runners? Because I needed one—not for them but for me. Sometimes a pithy little sentence is just what it takes to define ourselves and fall back on when we lose our way. *Keep pushing . . . always* is an amalgamation of Dr. David Livingstone's "Bash on, regardless," Bruce Springsteen's "Keep pushing 'til it's understood," and a little of Romans 5:1–5, which reminds us that "Suffering produces perseverance, perseverance produces character, and character produces hope—and hope does not disappoint us."

Keep pushing is a reminder not to settle but to dream, to live, to sing, and sometimes it's about letting go of the past to fulfill your destiny. I had tremendous guilt and regret over my wilderness years, and that guilt and regret ultimately wore me down. I needed to stop looking back and let it go so I could move forward.

Keep pushing is not about rituals, performance, accomplishment, achievement, or feeling guilty about taking a day off from the pursuit of a quest. It is a pursuit of that best possible version of ourselves, refusing to accept mediocrity, and waking up each day full of hope instead of fear. It's having courage, taking a risk, staying focused on the important things in life. And it's remembering that courage is not the absence of fear but the ability to press forward despite your fears.

And, ultimately, that's why I chose to pursue the Olympic quest. I was afraid of what lay ahead—of what kind of person I would be without competitiveness and my childhood dream of being an Olympian. Would I settle? Would I stop dreaming? I needed something to help me move forward despite my considerable fears. I needed to know, before I put that Olympic dream behind me, that I'd made a valiant effort to see it come true, rather than suffering the regret of letting it drift away like smoke. I needed to know in my heart that I had fought the good fight. And beyond that, I would find something in the good fight that would carry me into a new and even more fulfilling phase of my life.

Because *Keep pushing . . . always* is also a reminder that life is sometimes about letting go—even giving up a dream—without sacrificing the personal qualities that make those talents and aspirations possible.

That path took me all the way to the top of that mountain overlooking Lake Garda. I found the ruins of a fifth century castle, stood on the edge of the cliff, enjoyed a stunning bird's-eye view of the lake, and said hello to the hiker couple on my way back into the city. But I never found the Madonna.

Sometimes a single run can make your whole life come full circle—or maybe just make sense of the things you never understood. Like a spark plug gapping the arc between connections, that run banished my fears of settling. I didn't run to the top of that mountain so that people could tell me I was great. I ran to the top of that mountain because on that given day, at a time when I doubted whether or not I was capable of continuing the climb, a still, small voice reminded me that I would be unhappy if I settled for anything less than my best.

I chose to become the very best version of myself at that moment. Not exceptionally fast, not exceptionally gifted in the directional department, just a guy who wants to see what's at the top of the mountain—and on the other side.

I figure as long as I live each day with that sort of mind-set, whatever random fears I have of settling or letting mediocrity seep into my life will be kept at bay just one more day—even if it means depending upon three simple words to find courage when I have none.

PAY IT FORWARD

REASON TO BELIEVE

Hey, Marty, said a familiar voice.

I'd been trying to get Lance Armstrong on the phone for six weeks. My career depended on our conversation. My *real* career. You need to get that one last interview, my editor insisted all through August, as I rose before the sun each morning to pour words from my head onto the printed page. I couldn't turn in the book until I had one final heart-to-heart with Lance, but as my deadline grew closer, it became more and more obvious that he wasn't in the mood to return my calls—until, of course, he chose the worst possible moment to pick up the phone.

"Worst possible moment" can mean a lot of things, so maybe I am overstating my plight. But I don't think by much. I was steering a Ford Econoline van without air-conditioning up the 405 through rush-hour traffic on a hot September afternoon, on the way to my first race as a high school cross-country coach. Fourteen boys and girls packed the bench seats—some of them, judging by the way they vaulted up and over the seat backs to sit on their best friends' laps, openly violating California seat-belt regulations. They were giddy about the race they were about to run.

So was I. No. Better than giddy. I was a freak.

I drove with my knees, holding the phone to my ear with one hand, waving the other in a dramatic demand for silence. When that didn't work, I turned and mouthed *Lance Armstrong.* Just like that, the chatter and hysterics turned into a quiet reverence. My team watched me drive with one hand, take notes with another, and conduct a telephone interview with the world's greatest endurance athlete at seventy-five miles per hour, cell phone squeezed between ear and shoulder.

I will pause here to note that California has since passed a law making it illegal to speak on the phone while driving a vehicle. Those of you wondering why such legislation is necessary need look no further than the previous paragraph.

I digress. This adjunct to the writing life came about when my oldest son transferred to another high school in our town. I'd made a point to strike up a conversation with the athletic director. It was a brand-new school. Their sports facilities were still being built. I figured they might like a little free help.

I'd be very interested in giving your cross-country coach some assistance, I told the A.D., explaining that I was a lifelong runner and had raced in high school and college. What I didn't tell him was that I'd long dreamed of coaching distance runners and that for years, I'd even imagined training schedules and places where my phantom team would practice. I had a mental list of race-day strategy tips I would impart. I'd see a hill while out for a run on my own and think that it would be a good place for my future athletes to do ten or so repetitions. I had a passion for running and a body of experience I could pass on to others. Couldn't hurt to ask. Right?

We don't have a coach. Do you want the job?

And so it began.

In addition to writing the book—grappling with story structure, sleeping troubled, and speed-dialing Lance's office each and every day—I was ordering uniforms, leading group runs, and trying to find new runners. There were only four on the first day of practice, all of whom started walking before we ran a single mile. Basically, I was building a program on the fly. The forty days and nights between the end of the Tour and my book deadline, which coincided with the day of our first race, were hectic to say the least.

I didn't mind. I was head over heels for this new hobby of mine. And that's what I thought it was—a hobby. I would do it for a season, maybe two. Realistically, I was too busy for the job. I was an international journalist, always a phone call away from hopping on a plane. I was a *New York Times* best-selling author. My articles about distance running had appeared in all the running magazines, along with mainstream mags like *Sports Illustrated* and *Esquire*. I would bless these young people with my wisdom and then move on when Devin graduated.

What I would not do was act like the stereotypical high school coach. I swore not to yell *Listen up, people* or adorn myself in spirit wear. And I would never, ever drive a school van.

Lance and I talked for thirty minutes on the day I broke that vow. In that time, I pulled up to the course, parked, and mimed for my team to warm up. I hung up before they finished, hurriedly jotted notes, then phoned my publisher with the good news. Glowing with equal parts success and relief, I watched my runners jog to the starting line in their new uniforms. This delicate balancing act between my career and my hobby seemed to be working out just fine.

Then I felt something else. Call it one door opening and another closing. There is something innately human and wondrous about being the best possible version of ourselves on any given day. Sometimes, to get to that point, it is uplifting to watch others push their own limits, even when they're nervous, doubtful, and scared—as my runners were at that very moment. I realized that the inspiration I'd once found in Lance and a faraway bike race could now be found right before my very eyes.

I also knew that the coaching gig was much, much more than a hobby.

Fourteen years have passed since that day. Devin has graduated from college, Connor too. Liam is a senior at his university.

I am still the coach. I shout *Listen up, people.* I clothe myself in so much spirit wear that my wife calls it my uniform. I have driven that van all over California—albeit in a far more two-hands-on-the-wheel, seat-belt-mandatory fashion.

I am hardly too busy for this job. Every day, as I will for years to come, I tell people about the special young men and women who let me be their coach. I got to coach my own sons, growing closer to them in a way that I never would have had I not accepted that fourteen-year-old invitation. And I know the simple act of service that comes from sharing knowledge and helping others realize their dreams is infinitely more fulfilling than anything I've ever done in my life.

To be a runner is to learn continual life lessons. To be a coach is not just to teach these lessons but also to feel them in the core of your marrow. The very act of surpassing personal limits in training and racing will bend the mind and body toward a higher purpose for the rest of my runners' lives. Settling for mediocrity—settling for good enough—becomes less and less of an option. And with so many in the world all too happy to bask in mediocrity—settling instead of pushing—those who learn to be the best version of themselves know the secret to a full life.

As I push my runners to persevere and be optimistic and diligent, I recognize how much I need to follow my own advice. I am blessed to know my runners. They have sharpened the life lessons I passed on to them—and sharpened me in the process.

THE PRICE YOU PAY

You hear the phrase "leave it . . ." a lot in sports. Sometimes it's "leave it on the field" or "leave it on the court," but the gist is to give it everything you've got. The trick, I think, is giving it your all when you don't have anything to give.

Case in point: my junior year of college. Not a good time. I was transferring from a school in the Midwest to one back home, which meant not just a physical change of scenery but a semester of living in my parents' house after enjoying the freedoms of college life. As a runner, it meant a new coach and new teammates. Even more humbling, it meant a semester at a junior college.

My new coach's name was Tom Messina. Tall, wispy mustache, walked with a slouch, spoke with a veil of sarcasm. He couldn't have been more than five years older than me, but he knew his stuff. This was important. I'd had half a dozen coaches in my ten years of racing—one more if you count the year in Louisiana where I was self-coached. I knew what made a good coach and a bad coach, and I was extremely critical of those who didn't measure up. It was the entitlement of youth, because running was my everything. I pored over every magazine, every race result, every bit of running-related minutiae that popped up on TV or elsewhere in the media. I knew where I was when Frank Shorter won the Olympic marathon and where I got the news that Pre died. I disdained the neophytes who had embraced the running boom, turning running from an individual religion into something crass and pedestrian. I checked *The Jim Ryun Story* out of the school library so many times that I finally just hung on to it until the year ended. And I knew that nothing in the world made me calmer and more at peace than a forest path, a good stride, and no one to race but myself. That hasn't changed.

My coaches had ranged from Mr. Roberts in sixth grade, who saw my newfound passion and passed along *How to Train for Track and Field*, a simple act on his part that emboldened me to give up Little League baseball and dedicate myself to training; to the crazy Al Withers, who ran with the team and liked to leap high in the air to announce his flatulence; all the way to the horrible coach I'd had my first two years of college. It's funny how a single bad coach can wipe out years of growth and confidence provided by the great ones. By the time I transferred back home, my love of running was gone.

But I couldn't give it up. I had defined myself as a runner for so long that not being one terrified me. Without running I would be lost. My agent once called an editor of mine a guy "who behaved like a bad girlfriend" because he ignored me until I wanted to find a new publisher, then suddenly showered me with affection, making me think I'd be crazy to go anywhere else. Today I see running as a daily challenge that helps me transcend personal limits and reminds me of my hopes and dreams when I have let them slip away. But back then running was my bad girlfriend.

Anyway, what followed was a season of hard training, competitive ups and downs, and the awareness that I was running better than I had in a long, long time. Tom Messina made all this possible. He cajoled, threatened, listened, joked, yelled, and basically became the model for how I coach today. When I think about the reasons I have nurtured the belief that coaches can make a huge difference in a young person's life, it's because Tom Messina made such a huge difference in mine.

I was a mess the night before the last race of the season. My self-doubts and lack of self-worth had me spinning. I'd stepped off the track in a recent 5,000-meter race, and Messina had challenged me to either step up and race to the best of my ability or quit the team entirely. So I quit. Then I unquit. And there I was, a week later, unable to sleep because I had this make-or-break steeplechase to run the next day.

I called Messina. It was almost midnight. For an hour, he listened to me talk about those self-doubts and fears about the future, basically letting me download the litany of failed hopes and dreams that had left me, at twenty years of age, feeling like I was at a personal dead end.

"You have one of two choices," he concluded, reminding me that I needed to get my sleep. "Either the pain of suffering or the pain of regret. One lasts about ten minutes. The other lasts a lifetime. You pick."

Not try hard. Not find your happy place. Not even win. Just . . . suffer. Hurt so hard that you own the outcome.

Leave it on the track. Or be haunted.

How many times since, when I wanted to settle for something in between my best and something not so good, have I been reminded of those words? The sublime experience of pushing to the limit, whether in writing or parenting or just going beyond myself to be kind to some obnoxious soul I might otherwise be tempted to scorn, is infinitely better than phoning it in.

Suffering is not always about getting hit in the teeth by a baseball bat. Far more often it's about the mental struggle to hold on when life makes your head explode. Not quit. Not slow down. Just hold on. Keep pushing. Believing, in some strange and magical way, that you can do something that you and nobody else you know ever thought possible.

Today my runners gathered in a circle for our traditional post-workout cheer. Some teams put their hands in the middle and say "Team," and some say "Win," and some say their school's mascot or one of about a million different things. We say "Glory." I stole it from *300*.

The workout was hard and dusty, and everyone had that vibe about them like they just wanted to gossip a little, then go home and suck down carbs. So when we did the "glory" it had a lame, desultory feel.

I let them go. But after ten steps I called them back. I just couldn't let such a quality workout end on that powerless note.

To my surprise, they were thinking just like me. We didn't exactly boom it out that second time, but it was more cohesive. More about why we do the hard work. There's nothing blasé in how my runners shout "Glory" on the state meet starting line. They've said it a thousand times since June, and as they say it one last time before the final gun of the season, they are reminded of the places they've said it before—and not once has it been just a rote, monotone recitation but a call to suffering. That's why I called them back to do it again. This is the sort of little detail that becomes a big part of that midrace moment when they need to choose between suffering and regret.

Great races are not always defined by traditional notions of success. Did I start out strong the day after that phone call? Yes. I cruised that first lap in seventy seconds and felt smooth. Did I race well? Definitely. By the start of the bell lap I was in third place, poised to move up. Did I move up? Oh yeah. I came off the turn and powered down the backstretch, catching the second-place runner and looking for first.

But then my legs got stiff like logs. I tied up so completely that I could barely leap over the final water barrier. Leap would not be the proper term. I literally willed myself over the barrier and toppled into the water. I crawled on my hands and knees until I was back on dry track. Runners passed as I stood and hobbled for home. There was still one last barrier before the finish, and to this day I don't know how I hurdled it.

I staggered the final hundred meters to the finish and collapsed in the infield. I literally could not stand for five minutes.

Now, I have won many races. And I have known the cheers of the crowd. But to this day, that's my favorite performance. I gave that race my all. I left it on the track. That's why it was a success.

That day I said good-bye to my bad girlfriend and entered a wilderness that did not include my running shoes or that welcoming forest trail for four long years, giving a whole new meaning to "leave it on the track." This was a time I would regret more than any bad race, until the suffering actually got so bad that I needed to find a way out.

My teams are peaking and tapering right now. I see them struggling to be their best. I think of Tom Messina as I watch them find that sweet spot of the racing season, and I thank him for taking my phone call that night. I found strength in his words, even if those words empowered me to leave running behind until I found an identity beyond the sport. As my runners step to the line in these next crucial races, my prayer is that they cross the finish line with nothing left—that they leave it all on the course, even if it's a day where they feel they have nothing left to give. That attitude carries over into jobs, love, and any other daily decision to make the most of life.

Running won't always define them, but choosing the pain of suffering over the pain of regret most definitely will. My prayer is that it's a choice they—and I—will always keep on making.

EXCUSES, EXCUSES

To be an endurance athlete is to have a million excuses at the ready: It's too cold to train, too wet, too sunny, too Saturday. My shoes are wet. My tires are flat. I'm fat. I'm out of Gu. I can't put this book down. I just ate a burrito. My cat has a tumor. And on and on.

To coach endurance athletes is to hear a million more: I forgot my shoes. I have to go to the bathroom. I stayed up too late last night. I have to go to the bathroom. I think I might throw up. My mom's yoga teacher says that more than ten miles a week is too much. I have to go to the bathroom. And on and on.

I turn a deaf ear to the lightweight and overwrought, particularly the frantic need to pee for the tenth time in a single interval session. Let me restate that, at the risk of sounding heartless: Everyone has the choice to go, but I ask my runners to honestly gauge the urgency before making their decision midworkout. Just so we're clear.

Why am I so oblivious to these heartfelt pleas? Because back in the day, I was the King of Excuses. I know the real thing from a bogus imitation all too well. And I also know that there is no such thing as a good excuse. Excuses limit us and prevent us from being the best possible version of ourselves.

My high school and college training was defined by my singular dedication to skipping hard workouts. I always loved the feeling of winning, and I always loved trail runs on a sun-dappled afternoon, but something about track workouts got inside my head. I was the guy (*that* guy, the one every coach knows is about to pull the same excuse again) who got so anxious on speed days that I developed self-induced gastrointestinal distress. No workout was complete without a couple of trips to the outhouse—or the local bushes.

On race days it was worse. The butterflies would bounce around my stomach for a good twenty-four hours, churning everything I ate into a roux of nausea and dread. I would consider the many ways I might somehow be relieved of this panic flooding my body; anything to avoid having to toe the starting line and face the looming three miles (six in college) of full-tilt, unadulterated, anaerobic catharsis.

Still, racing held a therapeutic connection to validation and approval for me. That honesty and reckoning is why I got so nervous. I often say that the best runners race as if their parents won't love them if they lose. My runners think I'm joking, not knowing that I'm talking about myself. Who wouldn't be nervous about the prospect of failure and rejection?

In the end, races are hard, but they cleanse body and soul. Crossing the finish line is like walking out of the therapist's office. The French like to say that cycling's individual time trial is the race of truth. I think the same can be said of any competition that pits you against an obstacle—the clock, a mountain, your nerves, and, most of all, fear.

Excuses are born of fear. That's why I am a stickler for not allowing my runners to indulge in them. Need to throw up? Go right ahead, the trash can's right over there. Forgot your running shorts? Lucky for you, I have a drawer full of backups—just make sure you wash them before bringing them back. And as for that bathroom break . . .

I know firsthand that if you accept the excuse, it will eat into every part of your life. Once, I started a race and knew within a hundred yards that I just didn't want to be there. So I managed to trip over a tumbleweed that happened to blow across the course as I ran past. All that got me was a hard spill, tumbleweed stickers in my leg, and the suddenly brutal awareness that I still had a race to win and a pack of runners now fifty yards in front of me. I got off my butt and finished second.

Then there was the time in college that I invited a cute red-haired girl with pouty lips and an hourglass figure to the homecoming dance. Janet Something. Homecoming coincided with an away cross-country meet. So what did the excuse factory dream up? A shameful and glaringly obvious ruse. I packed all my running stuff in my travel bag, slipped into my uniform and sweats, then made sure my roommate saw me leaving my dorm room before the crack of dawn. Ostensibly, my destination was the athletic center two miles away. But the trail took me through a patch of forest, where I lay down to take a nap until I was sure the team bus had left without me, rationalizing my choice as I lay atop the damp, golden autumn leaves.

A month after the dance, I found out that Janet had a preference for Northern Michigan University Wildcats hockey players instead of 129-pound cross-country runners with hair halfway down their rear ends and no discernible biceps. Served me right.

You would think that homecoming would represent the nadir of my chronic excuse-hatching period (I still cringe about it almost thirty years later), but by then I was fully embracing defiance, declaring my independence by not being a runner anymore (this being the direct opposite of running for approval). Still another year followed of long bathroom breaks at practices, stepping off the track (twice) during races, and just a general drift away from commitment to developing my God-given talents. When I finished fifth in my final college race—perhaps the best steeplechase of my career—I retired.

I stopped running, but the excuses continued. Because I had nurtured the habit, I found ways to sabotage all areas of my life. My final excuse came when I was helicoptered off the course at the Raid Gauloises, an adventure competition spanning hundreds of miles. Often more than a week long, it was widely, and quite rightly, called the toughest race on earth. My injury seemed severe enough to warrant an extraction, but in retrospect all I had was severe dehydration, a dose of altitude sickness, and an abiding hatred for my teammates. The three months of what-if depression that followed was my own damn fault. I was haunted evermore by my inability to suck it up and get the job done.

I vowed never to let that happen again.

It's no surprise that I set aside adventure racing soon after, but not before returning to the next Raid and finishing the thing once and for all—all eleven days, seven hours, and forty-nine minutes of it.

My return to running was different the second time around, because I wasn't doing it for anyone but me. I held myself accountable for every race, every workout, and every last mountain. Correspondingly, my marriage improved, and I stopped feeling this inordinate need to find myself by traveling around the world to participate in countless different races. All of me that I needed to find was right here at home.

I know that my runners will continue to make excuses. That's part of being an endurance athlete. Who in their right mind wouldn't find excuses to escape an hour or more of suffering?

Excuses always lead to a reckoning. We find reasons not to take that first step out the door, just as we find ways to be—or not to be—our best. I strive to instill a no-excuses mentality in my runners. Weakness, doubt, and fear are parts of the human condition. Facing them instead of fabricating an elaborate ruse to sidestep them— hoping to avoid them but ultimately carrying them in our hearts and minds and psyche until they whittle away at our being—gives us a direct route to hope and dreams. Along the way, we reap all those other by-products that make the suffering a tonic for our souls.

NEW SHOES

New runners and their parents often approach me after the first practice, a sheepish look on their faces. "Um, we were hoping you could tell us what kind of shoes to buy," the parents will volunteer, making it easy on their young athletes. With so many makes and models on the market, buying a running shoe seems as exotic as piloting a container ship through the Panama Canal. They are asking, in specific terms, where to go, what to buy, and how to determine precise fit.

At least that's what they think they're asking.

What I give them is advice on how to enter into a serious monogamous relationship. Because, after all, that's what they really need to know. A footwear purchase is a harmonic convergence, not a simple act of commerce. They must know this as they slap down their credit cards.

But we've just met. And to say that aloud, at such a tender stage of our getting to know one another, would make me sound daft. So I tell them about shoes, parsing my words, doling out information in a way that will make them see the importance of what they're about to do. They will soon be introduced to terms like *Personalized Heel Fit, EVA midsole, Trusstic System,* and *GEL Cushioning.* Their heads will spin. They will be tempted to spend far more than they had planned. But the simple truth is that shoes are just shoes. All the performance features in the world won't make someone a better runner, unless that person actually puts the shoes on and steps out the door. Having said that, there is a shoe for every personality, matching an individual's aspirations with his or her physical and emotional abilities. Finding that match *will* make you a better runner.

I've preferred the Asics Gel-Kayano for about as long as I can remember. It's supposed to be a road shoe, lacking the sort of heavy-gripping tread pattern of a trail shoe. And I know that its lack of lateral support reduces its life span every time I scramble side to side down a ridgeline or do those quad-searing burpees and squat presses at the House of Pain. But I love them just the same.

Sliding my dogs into a new pair of Kayanos is like strapping a slender racing-striped pillow to the bottom of my feet. Even as the midsole breaks down and the ride gets a little more bumpy (*ride* is a very popular term among the shoe designing set), I love how the mesh upper stretches just a little so the laces fit more snugly. The typical performance life span of new running shoes is 350 to 400 miles. I don't keep track of how many miles I put on a pair of shoes, but I know they're through when my knees ache during a run, my hips are a little sore afterward, or the mesh upper becomes so frayed that the big toe on either foot pokes through.

When new shoes are purchased, the old pair enters into a refresh-ing new phase of our relationship: casual wear. The shoes I wear when I coach are always that recently replaced pair of Kayanos. Their coziness and perfect fit make them a guilty pleasure, as if I've found a way to wear slippers in public without looking like a man who has lost his way. Whether I am calling out splits at the start/finish line or racing up the back side of Mt. SAC's Reservoir Hill to cheer on a runner, they are my bellwether of comfort and support.

I am not alone in my passion. Runners get that way about their shoes. I think it's because they're the only true piece of gear a run-ner needs. A cyclist gets bedazzled by—and quietly judged by—not just his bike but also his Lycra, clip-in pedals, aerodynamic shoes, air-ventilated helmet, and even his half-ounce carbon fiber bottle holder. A golfer loses hours in magazines, researching clubs, bags, tees, balls. Once upon a time, a golf ball was just a golf ball. Now you can pick from any of a number of velocities and covers and arcs.

But to know a running shoe is to know that simple pursuit of simplicity and performance. When I first became a runner, the shoes themselves were suspect. Many believed that running shoes were just a clever marketing gimmick. My dad didn't believe in them at first, so he ran in his venerable Adidas gym shoes. This, of course, meant no running shoes for me. I trained in Pro-Keds with canvas uppers and chevron-grooved rubber soles the first three years I ran. My racing flats, when I finally bought some-thing more sensible to compete in, were the first-generation Onit-suka Tiger with the thinnest rubber sole imaginable and the sheerest of nylon uppers.

I'd jog the course before a race with one flat in each hand. When race time came, I'd change out of my Pro-Keds and into those flats. I could feel the weight differential immediately. I'd gone from wearing the equivalent of lead boots to featherweight secret weapons that spoke to me like a promise—a promise of victory.

Now when I watch my runners before a race, performing the same routine, I remember that heady sensation of feeling the weight disappear from beneath my feet. Speed beckons. I watch my runners prance like colts. One of them adds to the ritual by having me yank on the double-knotted laces, just to make sure they won't come undone. Those moments of mental fortification and routine are just as important to a successful race as any hill repeat we will ever perform in training.

How should a running shoe fit? There should be a thumbnail of room between the toe and the front of the shoe. No more. The front portion of the shoe, known as the toe box, should be roomy enough to wiggle your toes, but not so loose that your forefoot slides around when you run. The laces should feel snug, but not so tight that they cut off circulation on the top of your foot. And your heel should be cradled, not pinched.

All the other stuff that people spend so much time worrying about is just fine-tuning. There are shoes for overpronators, supinators, comfort and cushioning geeks, and those enviable runners with a perfectly neutral gait who could run a marathon in a pair of wooden clogs without suffering so much as a blister.

At least once a week I have my runners take off their shoes and run barefoot on a grass soccer field or on the sand down at the beach. This strengthens their feet by allowing their gait to return to its natural and primal state. They love the barefoot feel and the childlike freedom of letting their feet run naked, so to speak. But not all trails are soft and cushy. We live in a world of pavement, toxic muck that can cause infection, and forest paths mined with jagged rocks. Barefoot running is a fine diversion, but at some point it limits where they can run and how far they can go. Running shoes are a must, and the right shoe allows them to train anywhere, train faster, train farther, be less prone to injury, and feel more comfortable.

So how do I define the right shoe for my runners? That's not for me to say. I think the shoe finds the runner as much as the runner finds the shoe. Its look, fit, and performance level must match how you see yourself on the inside.

One of my runners was recently sold a pair of shoes that weren't quite right. The store recommended a brand that they had in surplus and were eager to dump. The boy and his parents were too new to the sport to know better. They thought all running shoes were supposed to fit like that. When he wore them to practice, I could see right away that the shoes were suited to someone with a different temperament. I know it sounds crazy. Maybe it's something like those soothsayers who profess to see the colors of a person's aura. But I can tell when a shoe isn't right.

I didn't say anything. The shoes were his, after all. They looked quite spiffy, with a shiny white upper and bright red stripes. But a month later, he suffered a stress fracture. That's when I found out they'd sold him the running version of clown shoes, with enough room between the toe and the front of the shoe for four thumbnail lengths. Something as simple as that affects a runner's gait immeasurably, putting pressure on the knees, feet, and hips in all the wrong places. When I searched the training logs for reasons he might have suffered a stress fracture, my conclusions came straight back to the shoes.

I made that runner go back and get the right shoes, in a style that suited his personality. Of course, it was too late to get a refund. The guilty shoes were worn and weathered. But I was thrilled when he showed up at the track in new shoes from a different store the next day, ones with a style and personality that matched the kid I knew.

Try it. You'll see. The shoe will find you. You don't need to know catalog buzzwords or possess an encyclopedic breakdown of the correlation between supination and structured cushioning foot-wear. You'll heft a just-out-of-the-box shoe in your hands, slide it on your foot, prance a few steps around the store, and you'll know. And then—voilà!—you'll have entered into a relationship, albeit one that ends in 350 miles or six months, whichever comes first. Then it'll be time to buy a new pair and commit to another all over again. It won't feel like love, but something very, very close.

A TIME FOR STRETCHING

In season, practice at the high school starts at 3:00 every weekday afternoon. I like to say that the start/finish line is our spiritual home, so I stand there and wait, studying my runners as they straggle out of the locker room and onto the track at precisely 2:58 or 2:59. They walk in ones and twos. Some of them are fully dressed and ready to run, but most carry their shoes in one hand. It's an oddity about distance runners that many wait until the last possible minute to stretch a pair of thin running socks over their bare feet and lace on their shoes. I did the same thing when I competed. Shoes imply commitment. The world of school or leisure is left behind, if only for a while. The workout has begun.

We start with an easy 800-meter jog. The runners plod around the track, gossiping and chatting about their day. It's a joke how slow they go, which is by design. I don't want anyone sprinting the warmup. Sometimes they call out to me as they pass, usually with some joke about a fake injury that will get them out of a workout. Sydney, the 800-meter runner who knows how to push my buttons, likes to tell me that she's going to quit and become a cheerleader.

"Good luck with that," I yell back.

She knows that I have nothing against cheerleaders but am adamant that those with the God-given talent to run like a Kenyan need to be in the arena, pushing their limits.

The same holds for the guy who promises to quit and join a steel drum band. And the superscholar who juggles choir and cross-country and says he can't figure out which is more important in his life. It's all part of the transition from the school day into the two hours of intense physical effort that is about to take place.

After the warmup jog, the team assembles on the track. Sometimes it's a circle, with the captains in the middle. Sometimes it's in five or six rows, with the captains up front. Then they do something that could loosely be referred to as stretching. If you have ever been to a football game and seen the pregame warmup, during which the players line up in precise columns and perform synchronized stretches, then you know what a proper stretching session looks like.

This is not that.

My runners face the wrong way, laze on their backs, and pretend to contort their bodies in a manner that prepares their muscles for the explosive movements of running. They break rank and form small circles, sharing secret truths. The girls admire one another's workout apparel or the way that someone's shoes might match her new singlet. They talk about homework, they talk about life, and they talk about the upcoming meets. I walk through them as they loll on the artificial turf, looking at their faces to see who's happy and who's tired and who's preoccupied with worry.

"Two minutes," I'll yell once I think it's been going on too long. I don't like this part of the workout to go longer than fifteen minutes. I think ten minutes is too much. Five, actually. To tell the truth, we don't need this part of the workout at all.

Physiology tells us there are two different kinds of stretching. There is static stretching, of the standard touch-your-toes variety. This is what my team is pretending to be doing. Studies have shown that static stretching does absolutely no good at this point in the workout. Afterward, when the muscles are hot, the slow process of lengthening and loosening is a vital part of the recovery. But at the start, it invites micro-tears and all other manner of avoidable injury.

Then there is dynamic stretching. This is the real stuff. Dynamic stretching is a series of movements like high knees, butt kicks, A-strides, B-strides, lunges, bounding, and other leaps and shimmies that do the most good before a run. The neuromuscular coordination of dynamic stretching invites the nerves, muscles, and both sides of the brain to have a conversation. The runners stand a little taller, as these exercises force them to stay up on their toes. Their hips come forward, their shoulders roll back, and their chins stop pointing at the ground. If this sounds like great running form, it's because it is. Dynamic stretching is a series of minor movements that constitute a great warmup but also train the mind and body to slowly but surely run more efficiently.

I read recently that stretching does no good. That it's just some sort of modern invention, courtesy of the running boom. I disagree. Stretching is primal. Watch a lion in the wild or even the family dog. The first thing it does upon waking is stretch its body, making bunched muscles grow long. I think there is some sort of oxygen release that takes place, something physiological that hasn't been noted that comes with a good stretch. To stretch muscles is to know a certain contentment. Maybe that's not the right word. All I know is that for my own fitness, stretching is last on my list of work-out priorities. It's like cleaning the backseat of my car: I put it off and put it off and put it off, then find the process rewarding once I finally force myself to do it.

At the end of a run, I like to trick myself into stretching and doing abs. I lie on my back in front of the TV, telling myself I am going to do nothing. But doing nothing is difficult. So I bend my knees and do a few crunches. Then I cross one leg over the other and pull my knees toward my chest, knowing that I will stretch my glutes, hamstrings, and hip flexors in the process. It feels good. So I do the other leg. Then I do some more abs, twenty-five pushups, and drop down into a plank position before pulling my knees up under my body and doing something very much like the Child's Pose from yoga.

Or sometimes I don't. This morning I ran, then threw on a pair of sweats and sat down in my chair to write. My hamstrings are now locked. It will take a half-mile of slow jogging at the start of my next run before they loosen up. As they regain their elasticity, they will initiate the top-down unfurling of the body. The calves and soleus and soles of my feet will slowly limber up, until I am finally ready to leave warmup mode behind and open up my stride.

Every time I abstain from stretching, I feel the little stretch Nazi in the back of my head, tut-tutting that I am deficient. Stretch

Nazis are people who think the stretch means more than the movement. That the lion gets more from the warmup than the hunt. The Bikram yoga instructor who was openly bemused midclass by the concrete inelasticity of my quads and glutes is a stretch Nazi.

"You must be a runner," she tittered, as if I had not yet attained the level of enlightenment enjoyed by the sweaty, stretchy men and women around me. They all turned, midpose, to stare.

To which I nodded, socially outcast for my tightness but relieved that I belonged to a tribe other than theirs. I struggled through the rest of the class, and never went back.

The way I trick myself into a postrun stretch and that slow trot to get loose may appear to represent the opposite ends of the stretching spectrum. But in actuality, they are the same thing: a transition. We think that stretching is preparing the muscles, when in reality it's a way for the mind to segue in and out of the training. The workout itself is a striving to be our best when mediocrity feels as far off as the North Pole. It doesn't matter how far or fast (or casually slow) runners run—the point is that they're doing something to be a better version of themselves. The transition in and out of the workout—the stretching—is how we ramp up and come down from that journey.

As for my runners, I know that static stretching does them very little good. But I also know from experience how vitally they need that time. They aren't relaxed like that during school, and they certainly aren't during the run. When I tried to cut out the static stretch a year or so ago, the whole vibe of the workout changed. It was all bad juju and disorientation. The runners needed the transition to prepare themselves for the work. I missed the banter. Worse, I had become my own churlish version of the stretch Nazi, which was not a good thing at all. So I put the stretch back in.

Too often I am consumed with being time-efficient in my coaching and in my own life, which can make something like stretching seem frivolous because it serves no direct, obvious purpose that can be time-quantified. In fact, stretching and time have about as much in common—to paraphrase Elvis Costello—as dancing and architecture. My runners have taught me that stretching is a state of mind. It is about personal flow and reconnection and a little bit of strapping on the mental battle armor for what's about to come next. It is about the transition from the outside world to the pursuit of personal betterment.

When I look at it like that, making time for stretching is not just calming, it is vital. I need to do that a little more often.

ICE BATHS

"Do we have to go in?" my runners ask. They always ask, no matter how many times we do this. Sydney, the blond with blinding speed, is the most vocal today. "Everyone," I respond, trying to look stern, thinking it will give them resolve. "All the way up to your hips."

"I'm just asking," she says, hoping to make me laugh.

"In."

I am sweating in the mountain sun. Trail dust coats my calves and shoes. I've just run Mammoth Rock with my team. It is my favorite trail in this mountain town, an out-and-back eight-miler that grinds uphill through a sage meadow, plateaus at a manzanita pasture, then climbs into a pine forest, through an avalanche zone of boulders and slide alder, and up to the gusty turnaround. From there I can look down on the funky off-kilter layout of Mammoth Lakes and gaze at the White Mountains a hundred miles due east in Nevada. But I never stop for long, because the wind blows hard up there, turning sweat into a chill within seconds.

The pace is always a chore on the way up, especially when I try to keep up with these teenage runners who can knock off six-minute miles and still carry on a conversation.

It's much easier on the way back. The stride opens up. The challenges are the roots and rocks jutting randomly from the trail. I can't count the number of times I've almost tripped, catching myself at the last minute. My greatest fear on this descent is landing so hard and so suddenly that I don't just scrape my knees or bruise my palms but slam teeth first into a boulder.

I run the Rock Trail whenever I'm in town, even in the winter if the snow is light. Before I became a coach, I ran the trail alone for more than fifteen years, dreaming of having my own team, planning the workouts I would have them run. Now, when I bring my team to Mammoth each August, the Rock Trail is always our first workout, its multiple ecosystems providing an introduction to the terrain we will come to know so well over the next week.

When we finally stride back down to Old Mammoth Road, the throttle wide open and every thought focused on that blessed moment when we will finally come to a halt, I introduce them to one more tradition: the ice bath.

The instant the run is over, everyone sits in an icy mountain stream for ten minutes. You have to keep your lower body immersed. That's the rule. Anyone who cheats, like the kid a couple of years back who sat on a rock so that only his feet were in the water, gets splashed by the rest of the team until that person is thoroughly drenched—so drenched that a deep shiver sets in, one that not even the mountain sun can thaw.

Much better not to cheat.

Green grass and smooth granite line the banks. My runners slip off their shoes and stuff the socks inside, then lower themselves gingerly into the water. I watch the action like a mother hen, looking to see who looks strong after the run and who looks beaten down. There is Sydney. There are the milers: Mabes, Kyle, and Sean. Lexi, the recent graduate, is on her way to Texas A&M and Division I cross-country. And then there's Colby, the pint-size freshman who seems made of nothing more than bones and determination. There are twenty in all. Some are new to the team, some are about to begin their fourth year.

A scream. An F-bomb. A gasp. They all make a noise as their toes dip into the water. The cold is punishing, and they clasp arms around torsos, as if hugging themselves could ward off the icy bite.

The current is clear and swift but not overpowering. They arrange themselves across the width of the creek, finding that sweet spot where the water is up to their hips but no more. The girls are braver than the boys at first, but it's the guys who soon dare each other to lean backward and fully submerge. The girls look at them like they're morons. In all my years of coaching, no girl has ever so much as put her shoulders underwater.

Then they sit, chattering about the run and about how their lower limbs are losing all feeling, and generally grooving on the shared experience. There's something about running eight miles at 8,000 feet of altitude that makes a team feel like they're doing something special. To follow that up with a mandatory bath in snowmelt, sure in the knowledge that the waters are fed by the massive mountain rising just over their right shoulder, only adds to the bonding.

"Can we get out yet?"

"No." It's only been three minutes, I tell them. You've got a long way to go. And get those hips in the water.

We do this to recover. When we get back home, we'll take ice baths in giant rubber garbage cans, which I will personally fill with Gatorade buckets full of ice cubes. Or they will go home and ice in their own bathtubs. An ice bath immediately reduces muscular swelling and inflammation after a hard workout. It begins healing the micro-tears and soothing tight calves and glutes. I think it's one of the most important parts of our training—just as important as the right shoes or hill repeats.

The principle behind all competitive running is finding that balance between the hard work necessary to reengineer a muscle so that it becomes stronger and faster, and the rest and recovery that allow sore and tired muscles to heal from that hard work. It's a curious fact that muscles don't become more powerful during the hard sessions but during the recovery. One tears down. One builds up. You have to go through hell to get to heaven.

Ice baths jump-start the process. When we finally get out of the creek, those muscles that were screaming about exhaustion and punishment ten minutes earlier will feel renewed.

"What about now?"

"Five more minutes."

Some days I get in the water, but this morning I sit on the grass and referee.

I need this recovery time, too. Badly. When I am not coaching, I am ruminating about the cares of the world. For months, I have woken up at 3 a.m. and been unable to fall back to sleep, trying to control things that I simply cannot. I mentally quote that verse in Philippians about not being anxious about anything, because God is in charge. But I do get anxious, even though I pretend I don't. My anxiety is like a mental workout, bruising my psyche the way the hills and miles of Mammoth torment my runners' muscles.

What they cannot possibly know is that running with them, and the daily discipline of coaching them, is my sanctuary. It's where I go to calm myself and pull back from whatever darkness or anxiety creeps, unbidden, into my day. The act of running and the focus on others instead of myself that is part and parcel of coaching soothes my psyche and keeps me whole. It is an ice bath, a good night's sleep, an easy day, a high-carb meal, an energy drink, a deep-tissue massage. Coaching, in other words, is the very best components of recovery rolled into one big bundle that keeps me sane.

"Coach, this water is so-o-o cold. Can't we just get out?" It's Sydney again.

"One more minute."

A lifetime of running has brought me a quiver of personality traits: self-reliance, perseverance, heightened mental and emotional awareness, and an unshakable reverence for pain and suffering. My runners absorb these qualities little by little every day that we train. They don't know it yet. And they have no idea how these traits will serve them in good stead when they race, and later, when they cope with bad bosses and mortgages and marriage and a million other stressors that can make a person crumble.

I know all this as I watch them goof in the water, its cold not even bothering them after almost ten minutes. I also know that my career struggles will eventually come to an end. That's another thing running teaches you: No matter how hard the pace or how high the hill, you will endure. Every struggle comes to an end if you just keep pushing forward.

That's when recovery begins.

"Time," I yell, already looking forward to tomorrow's ice bath. "Everyone out."

JUST ONCE . . .

Every August, on the first evening of our Mammoth Mountain training camp, I gather my runners in the small living room of my family's condo. They sprawl on the chairs and sofa and that seventies-era orange shag carpeting that we've never gotten around to replacing, eager for the freedom of being away from home and anxious about the hard miles in the week to come. Once they've quieted down, I pass out pencils and sheets of paper. Then I ask each runner to make a list of three dreams. One is personal, another is for the team, and the third is where they see themselves in ten years.

When the answers come back, the first two are inevitably all over the map—everything from achieving a specific time to beating a tough rival. But that last dream is a gut check, one that requires them to see the people they desire to become, exploring the parts of themselves they reveal to few people—and maybe not even themselves.

Right now, if you asked me to write down that sort of dream, it wouldn't roll off the tip of my tongue. You need to be honest with yourself and your desires, knowing in the back of your mind that controlling destiny is a fifty-fifty blend of aspiration and fate.

They fold their lists and turn them in. Later that night, when they have gone back to the team condos, I read them alone. Then I fold them back up and slip them inside the dirty yellow "2005 Le Tour de France" messenger bag that contains all my coaching paraphernalia. There the dreams will remain for three months, unopened and untouched. On the bus ride to the state meet the last weekend in November, I will walk down the aisle and hand back each runner's list.

By then the first two dreams will have either come to pass or be about to. But the third one will still be hanging in the ether. It's my wish that during the season they will have traveled so far as athletes and achieved so much that once seemed impossible, that they will have come to possess the building blocks of perseverance, determination, and grit that will guide them to the fulfillment of those final dreams.

Ten-year dreams are not simple. No one writes "I want to be rich" or "I want to be a movie star." Instead, they often combine several aspirations. Career, marital status, and financial health all make the list. So does a prayer or two. One brilliant young lady wanted to find a cure for Alzheimer's. But the thing that amazes me, year after year, is how many young runners write down that one of their greatest ambitions is to run a marathon.

Never mind that they can already perform the amazing feat of running three miles in fifteen minutes. Or a half-mile in less than two. A large percentage of my team feels they will not know true validation as a runner until they have run 26.2 miles. Their time has never once been mentioned—they just want to cross that finish line.

What I want to tell them—though I don't—is that the marathon is overrated. Finishing a 5-K, a 10-K, a half-marathon, or any event that pushes you out of your comfort zone is equally glorious. The marathon is just a distance, and a random one at that. When Pheidippides ran from Marathon to Athens in 490 BC to announce the Greek victory over the Persians at the Battle of Marathon, the distance was only twenty-five miles. That other 1.2 was added at the 1912 London Olympics so that the course would go past the royal box.

Most of us don't remember the royals, but runners do remember that Pheidippides shouted "Rejoice, we conquer!" upon arriving in Athens. He then keeled over dead from exhaustion, thus ensuring that people around the world would one day view re-creating his feat as the ultimate test of human endurance. It's interesting to note that his run from Marathon was his third long effort in three days—and the shortest of the bunch. Two days earlier, the herald had set out from Athens for Sparta, then continued on to Marathon, a distance totaling 150 miles, all run with great urgency, over rocky, mountainous terrain and under a baking-hot cloudless sky. The approaching Persian force was one hundred thousand strong by some estimates. The Athenian force was less than ten thousand.

So Pheidippides would have run very hard, knowing that the fate of Athens depended upon the strength and endurance of his legs. And he would have raced equally hard after the battle, eager to deliver the astounding news to a city that had been in danger of being wiped off the map. The Athenians had not just defeated the Persians, they had routed them. Only 192 Athenians died, compared with 6,400 of the enemy. This marked the first time in Greek history that their armies had defeated the Persians, then the scourge of the Mediterranean. The victory gave rise to the great Greek civilizations whose knowledge and democratic ideals would influence European thinkers and America's Founding Fathers centuries later. British historian John Stuart Mill would later say that the Battle of Marathon was as pivotal to British history as the Battle of Hastings in 1066.

So Pheidippides was not just running to deliver a message; he was proclaiming that the world had changed. A great seismic shift had tilted the axis in the Athenians' favor. I can just imagine him pushing the pace, his heart bursting with joy as he exulted in how it would feel to scream out the good news. Those legs and lungs of his, so broken and exhausted from the 150 miles he'd covered over the previous two days, tried to tell him to back off. Maybe find an aid station. Have a PowerBar.

But his adrenaline and endorphins overrode any practical thought. He must have known he was on the verge of collapse and death in those final miles, yet he pushed on. Nothing, not even life itself, mattered more than delivering that message.

So my runners and potential marathoners the world over understandably want to re-create this journey. It's the most famous running achievement in history. Okay, so how is running a marathon overrated? Certainly it's not from a historical point of view. To run the marathon is to join a brotherhood stretching back 2,500 years. What sporting endeavour offers that opportunity?

And it's definitely not overrated from the standpoint of personal validation. To cross the finish line of a marathon is to remind yourself that anything is possible, just so long as you keep putting one foot in front of the other and never, ever give up.

But that feeling of hope and triumph doesn't make you a better person. It doesn't take away your problems. It won't make anyone love you more. If you are running a marathon as a mark of greatness to be lorded over the mere mortal members of the populace, you're doing it for the wrong reason.

I think of how many athletes eventually get bored running marathons. They crave something more challenging, so they enter events like the Hawaiian Ironman and a hundred other races created to push competitors to a bold new Pheidippidian brink. A vast majority participate in these events for the sheer thrill of it. Another group just does it so they can tell people about it. That group of people, those who keep count of exactly how many marathons they've done or how many Ironmans they've completed, are missing the point. Soulless, joyless "accomplishment running" reeks of insecurity. Finishing an event is just a notch on the bedpost, so to speak.

I've been there. I ran my first marathon at seventeen because I felt that it would complete me as a runner, but I soon found that it didn't do the trick. I kept searching for fulfillment in other over-distance events like triathlons, adventure races, ultramarathons, and a whole bunch more marathons.

My turning point came one day in Patagonia, just moments before the start of the Raid Gauloises. There, on the shores of Lago

Nahuel Huapi, in the shadows of the snowcapped Andes, I recognized that the epic two-week race didn't terrify me so much as make me feel Sisyphean. I wondered when it would all end. When would crossing the finish line of yet another superhuman test of endurance make me feel complete? A still, small voice in my head reminded me that the time I'd been happiest in my athletic life was when I was just a runner. Just a guy who laced up his shoes and ran because it felt good. That was enough.

I haven't told my runners any of that. I probably won't. A coach can be a guide for many of life's paths, but some things you have to learn on your own. When they do choose to run their first marathon, however, I will tell them how to pace themselves. I will tell them not to slap five with all those nice redheaded kids lining the road, like they do in Hopkinton, because you will need that energy on the local version of Heartbreak Hill that is almost certain to be found at some point in all marathon courses (although sometimes that hill is a mental barrier instead of an actual climb). I will tell them to stay calm at the half-marathon mark, when a yip of inner jubilation tells them that it's all downhill from there. I will tell them that the marathon is never downhill. The last six miles will break your heart if you're not ready. You keep climbing, just like Sisyphus, until you reach the finish.

But when you cross that line . . . if you're lucky, it will come in a place like New York, where they hang a finisher's medal around your neck and random strangers will congratulate you on the streets like an old friend.

After finishing that marathon a few years back, I was hobbling the ten thousand blocks from Central Park to my hotel. That's the way it felt. How I forgot to carry cab fare, I will never know.

A crinkled silver emergency blanket was draped around my shoulders. I was already dreaming of the ice bath I would draw back in my room and how I would pour ibuprofen down my throat at six, perhaps seven, times its recommended dosage—anything to ease the cramping and stiffness already radiating up and down my body.

A mother and her very young daughter walked toward me on that narrow band of sidewalk. As I drew closer, aware that my shuffle and space blanket might be alarming to a child, I was unsurprised when the mother drew the little girl to her side. But as she did so, she turned her daughter's face to look at me. "This man did something very special today, sweetheart," the mother said, giving me a warm smile and congratulatory nod.

The little girl looked up—grinning, thanks to her mother's benediction, like I was some offbeat new sort of superhero, one with running shoes and bare legs and a race number and hair plastered to his skull by sweat and spongefuls of water, wearing a silver cape that he clutched about his shoulders for dear life with his right fist.

And, strange as it sounds, in the midst of my pain, I suddenly felt like one.

So, yes, finishing a marathon can be very special indeed. Perhaps just once, to see a dream come true.

ONE MORE TREE

Our Mammoth Lakes training camp is a bitch. We've gone every year since 2006 for a week of high-altitude training. And every year, I push the kids hard, making them run twice a day on mountain trails that always seem to go uphill. An average week is seventy miles of running.

For the seniors, it's an adventure they look forward to all year, second only to our Hawaii trip in terms of getting away from parental supervision and hanging out with friends. But it's not so easy for the freshmen. Not only are they running ridiculous mileage at seven thousand feet of altitude, but these young boys and girls just weeks removed from the eighth grade are stuck in a condo with a group of relative strangers. The routines and comforts of home are hundreds of miles away. Those seven days of running loom before them like a death sentence.

It's that way every year. Doesn't matter if it's boy or girl, freshmen have a tough time at Mammoth. No amount of team bonding exercises or communal ice bathing in the creek seems to make a dent.

This year, one of our freshmen was having that sort of ordeal. There was talk of wanting to go home. The athlete in question didn't know me well enough to trust me—to see that Mammoth has a purpose (it's about team building, not training) and that sticking it out would be a stepping stone to greater mental and physical toughness.

It all came to a head a couple days in. We were running the Rock Trail, a daunting climb through five riparian zones that offers stunning views of Mammoth meadow and just as many opportunities to embrace the suffering that comes with a three-mile climb and letting it rip down the three-mile descent. My buddy Hempy was one of the chaperones. He ran sweep, staying behind to make sure no one got lost. It's a safety precaution.

At one point, Hempy fell in behind the kid who was having a hard go of it. They struck up a conversation. The athlete let slip how he wasn't sure he would last the week.

Hempy is a marathoner and a scratch golfer. He could have chosen an analogy from either sport to set the kid's mind at ease. Thankfully, he chose running. "Sometimes when you run a marathon you feel like quitting," Hempy admitted. "So the trick is to tell yourself, 'I'm going to make it to the next tree and then I can stop.' But when you get to that tree, you tell yourself you can't stop until you make it to the *next* tree. And tree by tree, that's how you get through the race."

That became the mantra for the week: one more tree. When things got low, one more tree. When the week stretched too long, one more tree. When that last mile repeat seemed undoable, one more tree. When the group ran up the hill we call Devil's Sandbox to a turnaround point three trees up the mountain, that ideal became reality—claw up the ascent, on hands and knees if that's what it takes, one tree at a time.

Hempy's words did the trick. A new confidence arose from that runner. He made it through the rest of the week with apparent ease. I'd never seen that side of Hempy before, and it was truly amazing to watch.

One more tree.

It will get you through anything.

KEEP IT UP

In the Kevin Costner film *American Flyers*, which inspired me so much that I bought my own personal VHS copy way back in the eighties, the lead character is introduced to a special workout center whose motto is the Latin for "when you've got it up, keep it up." I will refrain from making the obvious connection, if only because it's too easy. All great double entendres should require a little effort.

Instead, that phrase got me thinking about a little concept known as vVO2 max. It seems that in France, at the University of Lille, a diminutive woman named Veronique Billat has revolutionized distance training. Dr. Billat discarded the traditional belief in VO2 max as a predictor of endurance success, adding a small *v* for *velocity*. Instead of focusing on oxygen volume (VO2 max), she believes that the key is the velocity that produces the maximum possible rate of oxygen consumption (vVO2 max). In other words, when you get it up, keep it up.

I had never seen photos of Dr. Billat until recently, but I envisioned an elfin woman with wire-rimmed glasses and a laboratory coat. She would look, in other words, very much like my sister

Monique, if only because their first names rhyme. You know how it is when you make those random connections. So imagine my surprise when I did a Google search and discovered that she looks just as elfin as I'd pictured, only without the glasses or lab coat. The two available photos show a rail-thin lady with a mischievous smile, performing some sort of test on athletes at a road race.

I think I'd have a mischievous smile, too, if my research had upended years of accepted physiology. The fact is, Dr. Billat's theory works. Runners employing her vVO2 max workouts see performance increases almost immediately. Not only does the ability to run long at speed become enhanced, but other key factors like lactate threshold and running economy get better as the workout goes longer. This is that magic bullet that any runner can access to get better. And here's the kicker: vVO2 max training pace is easy. Not Barcalounger easy, but relatively sedate on the intensity scale. Roughly put, it's the speed at which one would race two miles. If you don't want to do a two-mile time trial to figure that out, take your mile time, double it, and add eighteen seconds.

The classic Billat vVO2 workout is to run three minutes at this pace (or an 800 on the track, for consistency), then "float" for three minutes at half that speed before rocking right back into the interval. Ideally, it should be repeated five times. If the distance covered in those three minutes becomes less and less, stop the workout. I like to have my runners run an 800 at vVO2 pace, then jog a 400 in the exact same time interval for a one:one work/float ratio.

All right. So far, so good. But then Dr. Billat proved that the same gains can be achieved with just thirty seconds of running at vVO2 pace, followed by thirty seconds of floating. For me, three minutes is a long time to be working. It makes me reluctant to step on the track when I know that I will have to do 800 repeats, with all the mental and physical duress they imply. But to go thirty on and thirty off seems like cheating. It seems like one of those Jeff Galloway workouts where he tells people to take walking breaks in the middle of their long runs—effective yet somehow against the rules.

So I put it to the test, almost by accident. I got to the track half an hour before practice one day a few months back. I was grouchy because I hadn't run, and I knew that I wouldn't fit it into my day unless I tiptoed out into the dark later on—which I knew would never happen. Standing there at the start/finish line, the spiritual home of all runners, it dawned on me that even thirty minutes of effort was better than none. And so what if I wasn't going to get the hour I'd hoped for earlier in the day? The point was to do something.

I jogged a lap. It felt pretty good. But if I was going to trot around and around the track for half an hour, I'd get bored out of my mind. I'm convinced that the reason I've been a runner almost all of my life is that I don't log miles on the track and I don't run on the streets. It's all trails all the time, unless I'm doing specific speedwork on the track or I'm in a place like the Bahamas, where trails just don't exist.

Thinking that there was no time like the present to enhance my vVO2 max, I locked into something resembling two-mile pace and strode hard for 200 meters. But I raced too fast. There was no float to be had in my recovery interval. A Billat maxim states that there's no point in going faster than vVO2 pace during one of those sessions, because it can actually be detrimental.

The next 200 was more relaxed. I found my float on the recovery 100, and it was all good. I repeated the whole thing again and then again and then again. The workout felt easy, even after six or seven intervals. My heart rate was definitely up. Sweat soaked through my shirt and was making inroads down my shorts. My stride felt automatic. As the team shuffled out of the locker room to begin practice, more than a few were amused to see me doing speedwork. My pace was pedestrian by their standards, though they were kind enough not to say so. They did, however, stand at our spiritual home and bark out the same commands I yell to them: *Pick it up, Run tall,* and the ever-popular *Get serious, please.*

I'm methodical in how I train my runners, planning their mesocycles and microcycles and macrocycles months in advance. But with my own training, I am far more random. So I don't know if Billat sessions will yield the three percent increase in lactate threshold and six percent increase in economy over a nine-week span that she found with her subjects. All I know is that I can get in a quality session in a short period of time, and I enjoy the sensation of running fast and feeling my body respond positively. Most of all, her workout doesn't feel like one of those horrendous interval sessions that breaks my body down for days to follow. I don't like to think of myself as getting old, and I don't like to admit that standard rules of endurance apply to me (particularly the one that says the older you get, the longer it takes your body to recover), because I am both vain and stubborn. But I am willing to recognize that the morning after 10 × 400 at an all-out pace, I limp around the house like I have arthritis in every joint south of my navel. My feet ache, my Achilles feels like it's snipped in half, and I am as bow-legged as a bareback broncobuster.

Not so with the vVO2 session. It's nice to have a go-to workout that is guaranteed to work when time is short. My goal when training my runners is that they feel successful each and every day. That's how I feel when I run at vVO2. I'm not sure why, but I do. Maybe it's because the delicate physiology of running in that zone allows me to get it up, speedwise, and keep it up.

I still have that copy of *American Flyers,* though I no longer have the VHS deck that would allow me to watch it. The entire movie revolves around the powerful theme of pushing limits for as long as possible—to the point where the words challenge not just the characters in the film but the audience to never settle for personal mediocrity or second best. In the film, the double entendre Latin phrase is emblazoned on a T-shirt.

A shirt like that would be nice to have. It would be a reminder that racing fast is a choice, founded on the principle of getting up to speed and staying up to speed for as long as humanly possible. But I fear the euphemism would overwhelm the intended sentiment, and a grown man wearing a shirt like that around high school runners would seem desperately inappropriate.

It would be more clever—and more mysterious—to own a shirt emblazoned with the Latin for "vVO2." All great double entendres should require a little effort.

HILLS

Not long ago, I stood along the course as my wife ran a local race. I positioned myself at the bottom of the route's only climb, a 400-yard behemoth that twisted and turned and only got steeper before the summit. As runner after runner turned a corner and got their first glimpse, the reaction was inevitably a mixture of fear and despair. And to a man and woman, they used the exact same word to punctuate their dismay. In my whole life, I've never heard so many mild-mannered people drop a spontaneous F-bomb.

I know that feeling—that late-in-the-race, my-legs-are-dead, how-in-the-world-can-I-make-it-without-walking terror. And I've certainly decorated my share of courses with spontaneous outbursts of the world's most versatile word. But I also believe that hills get a bad rap. A guy like me, who needs a serious gut check once in a while to make sense of the world, needs hills the way I need the love of a strong woman. They kick my ass, keep me honest, and make me a better man.

They complete me.

Hills are the scourge of the running world, a place of private inward pain and challenge where all runners are equal, forced by the incline and their own relative fitness to become a better version of themselves on their journey to the top. Listen to a group of runners discuss some recent racecourse or group run, and the talk will invariably turn to the hill that tormented them all.

I was once on a bike ride with a large peloton of accomplished riders. The route took us inland from the Pacific, through the suburbia of Irvine and Tustin, out into the unincorporated wilderness of Santiago Canyon. The pace was uncompromising. What began as a friendly two-hour Saturday morning spin became quietly competitive. Nobody said as much, but we sized each other up with every pedal stroke, trying to figure out who was strong and who could be broken.

Just outside Tustin, the road pitched downhill for a mile. No one eased up. We used the time to gobble half a PowerBar and knock back a few swallows from the water bottle—anything to top off glycogen stores and provide the body with access to immediate power.

At the bottom of the grade was a sharp right turn. From there we would climb almost two miles up and over the canyon entrance on a wispy two-lane country road. The length and steepness of the climb was bad enough, but we all knew it would get much worse. Somebody at some point would force the pace. The race would be on. An easy group ride would become a test of fortitude and fitness, searing the lungs and turning quadriceps to jelly. That's just the way it is with hills. So as we pedaled into that turn, knowing what was about to come, our moods turned inward, waiting.

We began climbing. You could hear gears shifting and low grumbles. Finally, one guy said what we were all thinking: "This is where it gets bloody." And then, of course, it was on.

Hills are like that. And the best part is: Everyone bleeds.

That's why I love them. No matter if I am fit, fat, tired, exhausted, fresh, or thinking thoughts that take me a thousand miles away, the hill will have its way with me. I must confront the hill and, in doing so, challenge myself not to walk or turn around and head back down, and maybe even to sprint a little, if only to see if I am able.

The school where I coach rests in a mile-wide valley. Standing at the start/finish line on the track oval, I can look to my left and see a steep switchback trail up to a ridgeline that zigs and zags down to the ocean. Looking to my right, I see a series of low hills that rise and plunge in deceptively steep fashion. Their folds act as rest intervals in the midst of a hard run, the smooth dirt trails providing the perfect place to fly downhill without bruising the body.

I give every hill a name: Gazebo, Goliath, Devo, Triple M, Crazy Horse, and so on. A sample workout description might go something like this: "Run Scenic One, Scenic Two, on up to Falcon, down Triple M, out to Ladera Playground, and back up Crazy Horse." What might sound like gibberish to an outsider elicits a low groan from my runners. That particular loop is a telling test of strength. Some of those hills are long, some are short, and Crazy Horse climbs for a solid half-mile before it kicks a hard left up a series of dizzying switchbacks that have made one runner cry and more than a few hurl their lunch. But hills are a fact of life. Rarely a day goes by when we don't climb. And each time we do, those hills make us stronger.

The first time I tell new athletes to run Gazebo, which is three-quarters of a mile of what feels like pure vertical, they look at me for signs that I'm joking. But I'm not. So they trot out there and take their first tentative tour of her slopes anyway. It's steep right from the start. Small talk ends immediately. What follows is a good five to ten minutes of quiet introspection as they battle the urge to walk and lift their heads in vain, eyes gazing upward in a futile search for the summit. But that summit is not visible from any point on the climb. Only when you come around that final switch-back and see the cattle gate where a group of heaving runners is already waiting do you know that you have reached the top.

I like that process a whole lot. As a coach, I can actually see the mental transformation that occurs when a runner overcomes a phys-ical obstacle like a mountain. The world seems a little more manage-able. The athlete begins to believe he can meet that next challenge. Those legs, which felt so tired and weak at the bottom, unsure if they were up to the task, are now throbbing pistons. The lungs begging for an extra scrap of oxygen just moments earlier now bang like the stoker on a steam locomotive, throwing coal into the furnace so that the big engine—the heart—can provide maximum power.

There's a big reason the Kenyans consider hill running one of their primary forms of training. They talk about the explosive power and muscle tone they develop in their glutes, hip flexors, calves, and hamstrings. They talk about how their form becomes more precise, because the body needs to flow in an optimal fashion charging uphill—and when it's not, it's obvious. But they also talk about the way an hour sprinting up a hundred-meter hill twenty times increases their overall speed and cardiopulmonary function. As much time as my runners spend on hills, I don't think I've asked enough. If I could pick just one workout to build great runners, I would direct them to the nearest dirt hill.

Hills galvanize my soul. Many are the days I don't want to accompany my team. I figure I'll lag behind and make a good show of logging the miles. But I can never do only that, because at some point I feel incredibly lame standing around in my running shoes and shorts while my guys and girls head out for the trails.

What I'm afraid of is never the distance or even the speed. If I am honest with myself, I know that the days I want to hang back are the days when I've prescribed a serious dose of hills. I am afraid of Devo. I loathe Gazebo. Monica's Hill is hardly the sedate mesa the name implies. And Big Easy is big but hardly easy. To run them is to know that I will suffer. I will be forced out of my comfort zone. And I will have to compete, because as my runners get faster up those hills, I know that I am too vain to let them drop me.

But once we've gotten bloody and the trail has pitched up, forcing me to lean into it, keeping my arms low to stay relaxed and my chin tilted up to increase oxygen flow, it's kind of like going to church. Not church in the cathedral-of-nature sort of way but church in the manner of saying the Rosary or reciting rote prayer. In their way, these forms of church are a meditation. The constant repeating to oneself is calming, shutting out the outside world and making room for God.

Watch yourself next time you undertake a long climb. Even if you're running with a group, there's no place for chitchat. The mind turns inward. The outside world, with all its frantic busyness, is replaced by the here and now. What matters is the simple pursuit of being your best—not walking, not letting the place slack, and maybe just chugging slowly up the hill, one cruel step at a time, until it is done.

I give my runners lessons in hill running all the time. On downhills, I tell them to lean into the slope and get up on the balls of their feet. Running heel-toe acts like a brake and hastens muscle fatigue (laboratory scientists often induce fatigue by having subjects perform downhill running).

For uphills, I talk about the importance of the arms staying low and relaxed as they climb, never coming across the body or riding high like a sprinter's. The important thing is to quiet the upper body so that every bit of big engine horsepower pours into the legs. At the bottom of every hill, on any course, my runners will hear me yelling "ten quick steps." And then I watch as their cadence powers up to light speed for those powerful ten. It has made a marvelous difference, no matter the length of the hill. "Ten quick steps" is a nice way of saying "change your outlook" or "calm your fears." You take the fight to the hill at a time when the natural tendency is to slow down and hold a little something in reserve. "Ten quick steps" is the antidote for "This is where it gets bloody."

I search for hills to run, no matter where I'm traveling. Last summer I spent a week at a family reunion in South Dakota. There was not so much as a bump in the endless acres of corn and sunflowers. I ran gravel farm roads, past cattle pastures and the occasional pheasant. It was gorgeous and churchlike in its own way, but without hills, my runs didn't feel quite right. Maybe it's just the way I'm wired: I like confrontation, and hills are nothing if not confrontation.

Just the hill and me. Just the challenge and me. Just my fears and me.

Bring it on.

SLOW GOING

"I saw you out running the other day," said the woman. She was the assistant coach at a rival school. Even such a simple statement was fraught with competitive overtones.

I racked my brain, trying to remember where I'd run in the past week. Where—and how fast. "Yeah?"

Her face remained impassive. Perhaps I was imagining it, but I swore I saw the tiniest little smirk lift the corners of her mouth. "You were climbing the Live Oak Trail on Sunday."

Arrgh. I remembered. Feeling contemplative and nursing a food hangover from too much pescatore with jalapeños in pink cream sauce the night before, I'd specifically chosen to run the Live Oak Trail that day. Nobody runs there. Live Oak is a judgment-free path that starts in a narrow box canyon and climbs for a thousand meters, its switchbacks aligning themselves with the contours of the land. The view from the summit is one of the best-kept secrets in my neck of the woods, a 360-degree panorama that lets me gaze at the green slopes of Mother Saddleback in one direction and Catalina Island in the other. This is not a run to be hurried. I give myself permission to savor each footfall at a sort of dawdling pace barely faster than a walk. These are my most personal runs, ones that have nothing to do with speed or ego or even fitness. They're where I go to pray and create and self-examine. So why was I embarrassed about being caught in the act?

I deflected her comment, and we moved on to talk about how empty the trails can be on weekdays, when you feel like you're the only person out communing with nature. But my insecurity nagged at me long after we'd parted. I thought of a C.S. Lewis quote: "If one could run without getting tired, I don't think one would often want to do anything else." Which is exactly how I feel when I run slowly. As much as I love speed, I need the leisurely dawdle a few times a week. Those runs keep me fresh.

When new runners come out for my team each June, slow is their only speed. To build their endurance without causing injury, I send them out for short runs punctuated by walking breaks. After a couple of weeks, I urge them to stop walking and focus on completing an entire three- or four-mile run. The speed isn't important. What matters is the feeling of success that comes from making it through the entire workout without stopping. Slipping back into a walk is like a skip in the record, a bathroom break during a tight play-off game, a phone call during a first kiss. To be a runner is to run.

That success builds upon itself. I rate the success of each and every workout by whether or not my athletes feel a sense of accomplishment. That applies to every training session every day. If a runner slumps home beaten down, frustrated that his hard work isn't making him faster or that he's utterly failed because I asked him to run a split or distance beyond his reach, then I have failed, too.

One way to atone for my failure and keep the workouts fun is to schedule slow days. I don't call them slow days, because that term dictates the pace just as surely as do terms like *tempo* or *interval*. Instead, I want my athletes to experience the joy of setting out and finding a rhythm all their own. So I call these adventure runs. They are, perhaps, my runners' favorite sessions.

An adventure run means the runners pick the course and stay together as a group. I don't tell them that these runs nurture team bonding or that these are the runs they will remember most from their high school years. I just bring them all together on those days when their eyes have that hooded dullness of the mentally stale, then announce that today is an adventure run.

The next time I will see them is an hour or so later. Their shoes will be wet from wading across Trabuco Creek once or twice. Their knees and the palms of their hands might be muddy from scrambling up some berm in search of a trail. The boys tend to bring back sticks, vestigial trophies from childhood. They've used them as an impromptu sword or walking stick and feel compelled to keep them.

Very often the girls bring back a bouquet of wildflowers, presenting me with a daisy or some other plant whose name I do not know. I slip the flower behind my ear, because I am touched and want them to know how much I appreciate the offering. Many is the day I've stopped at the grocery store on the way home, having forgotten all about that little adornment. To say that I get odd looks is an understatement.

Every adventure run is different. Obstacles and mileage are never the same. The trail is always unique, taking the runners through orange groves and subdivisions, sometimes all the way to the ocean and back. Sometimes there is no trail at all, just some vast meadow they've charted like modern-day explorers.

The one constant among adventure runs is the euphoria on the runners' faces. When they return, they are not breathless and exhausted but refreshed. Whatever hardship I throw at them the next day will be more easily overcome.

When I run slowly on a trail like Live Oak, I'm having an adventure run. So why am I embarrassed? All the ego and veneer I build around myself to keep away the world is nowhere to be seen on one of my long, slow runs. I am stripped of ambition and pride, plodding along without getting tired and feeling in no hurry to run one iota faster. I am so vulnerable, it's as if I am running naked.

I spend a lot of time thinking of ways to push personal limits. I want to live a full and happy life, but sometimes it's not about doing more or going faster. Sometimes it's about slowing down just enough to feel and think and pray. A personal adventure run is all part of that process. Like my runners, the best days for me to go slow are when I am beaten down and need to feel a moment of success.

And that's nothing to be embarrassed about.

TIME TO RACE

Time to race. Finally.

I am up at 5 a.m. A quick shower in the dark as my wife sleeps, then I slip into my race day uniform: running shorts, black T-shirt, and over that a cardinal polo with the cross-country logo embroidered on the left side; running socks; and an aging yet extremely comfortable pair of Asics Gel-Kayano running shoes with more than 600 miles on them. I laid out everything the night before, like I did with my racing uniform back when I competed. That was almost forty years ago. I am just as excited now as I was back then.

I tiptoe downstairs and grind coffee, then unlock the front door into the cool morning air. The predawn smells like summer, all dried grass and dust, with just a hint of autumn. Nothing I can pinpoint. I pluck the *Los Angeles Times* off the driveway, then turn in a slow 360, scanning the starlit skies. Orion hangs low in the eastern sky, making its first appearance since spring, but there are no signs of rain. It's going to be a perfect day for racing.

Back inside I read the paper just long enough for the coffee to brew. I search in vain for mention that this morning is the opening meet of cross-country season. I am not surprised. Cross-country will never get the headlines. Even the occasional mention in the agate's fine print is surprising. It is as if there's some presumption on the part of editors that this sport exists far outside the mainstream. In fact, more athletes will compete in this one contest than in any sporting event this weekend. More than a hundred schools will attend. Thousands of spectators will line the course. Each runner's sweat, suffering, and desperate internal battles will go unchronicled. The only glory they will know is the self-satisfaction of pushing past preconceived personal limits. The race will be— *must* be—enough.

My phone, sunglasses, and car keys are waiting by the front door, where I placed them last night. I grab them on my way out.

The team's pop-up canopy rests across the back two seats of my Suburban as I make the right turn on Alicia that will bring me to the invitational. I live at one end of Alicia, and the meet is at the other. I haven't tested the theory, but I'm fairly sure that if I put the Rover in neutral at the corner of Alicia and Olympiad I could coast the next six downhill miles to the race. Later in the season there will be meets that require six-hour van rides and overnight hotel stays. There will be chaperones and time schedules and meal stops and interminable rides home, after the expectation of competition has been replaced by the parsing of results and hard reality of winning or losing. But on this first day of the season, I sleep in my own bed and drive myself.

I drive in silence. Hot coffee burns the back of my throat with every nervous gulp. I revel in the quiet, the darkness, and the hope that all thirteen weeks of summer training will yield a bumper crop of champions. The road is empty. I slip in a Springsteen bootleg and turn the music up as loud as I can bear. Adrenaline courses through my veins. My cares are forgotten. I am alive.

My goal is to be the first coach to arrive, so that we can get a prime area to set up the team canopy. I am successful. Slinging its eighty pounds over my shoulder, I march through the predawn silence to the same patch of grass where we set up last year. It seems like a small thing, but team canopy location has an effect on morale. Get there late and we end up making camp in a swale or hundreds of yards from the starting line. Get there early, before the other dozens of teams that will soon be clamoring for prime real estate, and I have my pick of the most level patch of green grass, with the best drainage and (I hope) well removed from the traffic lanes of runners and spectators who will soon flow back and forth over the course in a fluid continuum of humanity until the racing day is done. There is an element of feng shui to the logic. The canopy is that calm amidst the storm. Setting just the right vibe is vital.

All around me, as I set up the team area, I can hear but not see race officials making last-minute preparations: unfolding scorers' tables, plugging in power cords, prepping the snack bar. Another coach arrives and sets up his canopy twenty yards from mine. Rich Gibbs and I know each other well and have not seen one another since track season. But we just grunt a quick good morning. Another coach arrives. Then another. Soon the sun is rising, and the grassy field lining the course is a medieval carnival of multicolored canopies. Tarps cover the ground beneath them. Coolers of ice water and Gatorade are wheeled into position by eager parents.

The runners themselves arrive in ones and twos, nervous but eager to race. The 5:30 a.m. patch of empty grass is a portable city by 6:30. Coaches pore over race schedules as runners gossip or plug in earbuds to shut out the noise. Parents look on helplessly, not sure what they can do or how they can do it, but eager to show moral support for the team and their young runner. My two assistant coaches arrive, dressed just like me. I have always rebelled against wearing uniforms, as if it somehow threatens my creative instincts. But I like how my coaches and I look and the spirit of cohesion it displays to the runners.

The sun is still hidden by a gray marine layer that keeps the morning cool but humid. At 6:45 sharp, I gather my team to prejog the course. Studies have shown that the mind has a survival instinct which causes the brain to convince the body it's tired before true muscle fatigue has set in. However, if the mind knows the route and distance and what's around the next corner, that instinct is held at bay. So we routinely prejog the entire course, studying the hills and turns for strategic purposes, even as we quiet the part of our subconscious that would spread doubt at a point in the race when we need strength.

The first race starts at 7:45. The crack of the starter's pistol—the first of hundreds I will hear through the season—fills me with electricity. I am reminded of the unforgettable quote from *Top Gun*: "I feel the need for speed."

I love this moment. I love this day. I love this sport.

The meet is over by noon. I have spent the morning sprinting about the course during each race, yelling encouragement and strategy to each runner. My behavior could be considered manic, even by the rabid standards of a cross-country meet. The new runners on my team, the ones who know me only as the laid-back coach from those long summer miles, are startled. They shoot me a midrace look that says I'm possessed.

Some very successful coaches speak softly to their athletes as they run past. Maybe someday I will be like them. But for now I am who I am, the coach who demands very loudly that his athletes get up that hill right now, while in the next breath screaming that they are awesome and they can do this. Then I am sprinting off that hill, cutting a tangent to some other demanding section of the course, to wait for those same runners so I can yell more and probably louder. I want them to know how much I believe in them. My reward comes after each race, when an athlete walks toward me with a medal draped around their neck and a grin as wide as the Pacific spread across their face. "Look," they always say, "I won a medal. Can you believe it?"

Yes, I can.

THE MECCA

I stood atop Reservoir Hill, on a patch of dry grass alongside one of the most famous dirt trails in all of running. My varsity girls would soon be racing past. As spectators and coaches are prone to do at a cross-country meet, I'd sprinted up the hill to encourage them. "Dig," I was getting ready to tell them. "Pass three people right now."

From the summit, there's just a half-mile to the finish. It's the last of Mt. SAC's three legendary climbs, and there's not much gas left in the tank when runners get there. "Three minutes left," I would yell at them. "You can do anything for three minutes."

My cell rang. It was a childlike voice on the other end. I mistook it for that of my ten-year-old, who likes to call and tell me that he is bored.

"I'll call you right back," I said, cutting off the caller. One of my girls was hitting the crest. The others would soon follow. I stuck my phone in my pocket and yelled like a madman, surprising even myself with the sort of cold fury I could muster when I'm trying to sound inspirational.

I called back once the girls had all passed. Devin, my oldest son and one of the runners on my boys' team, answered. Dev's voice is usually cool and noncommittal. Yet now he sounded like a child. It turned out that he was the one who had called.

We talked for thirty seconds. No, fifteen. That's all it took. Fifteen seconds I will cherish forever.

Cross-country is the purest form of endurance competition: no time-outs, no halftime, no substitutions. There is just one discipline: running. Everyone races the same distance. Everyone suffers on the same course. It is one of the most widely watched sporting events you will ever attend, yet cross-country races never make the paper, giving the competitions a purist mentality. You compete because you love it. Not because you're going to get famous.

The greatest cross-country meet of all (and, it should be noted, the most overlooked by television and print media) is the Mt. SAC Invitational. Mt. San Antonio College in Walnut, California, hosts the two-day, 103-race event, which rightly claims to be the biggest such meet in the world. More than 25,000 athletes compete. The course is legendary and has changed little in the event's sixty years. Cross-country geeks young and old compare their times and war stories across the decades, content in the knowledge that—despite any generational gap—they have been tried and tested on the very same terrain.

The course begins with a bit of seduction, two mostly flat loops around a large pasture. It's easy to go fast, but runners do so at their peril. For at precisely the first mile mark, the course suddenly careens upward for 300 yards. These are the legendary Switchbacks (say "switchbacks" to anyone who has run Mt. SAC, and you will invariably witness a rolling of the eyes and nodding of the head, followed by a story of pain and misery), and they are followed immediately by a screaming half-mile of downhill. A few hundred yards of flat pavement later, it's back up ultrasteep and deceptively long Poop-Out Hill. The two-mile mark comes shortly after. Then it's up the straight and steady incline of Reservoir before once again charging downhill, only this time to the finish.

I first raced there in 1978. To return as a coach for the first time in 2005 was like stepping back in time, into a hallowed memory that had somehow remained unchanged. My team struggled that first year I coached, but being back at Mt. SAC gave me goose bumps just the same.

I tried to explain this attraction to Devin. He was not on my cross-country team at the time. Dev was a lacrosse player. He prefers hitting people with a stick to running up and down hills. But out of curiosity, he listened to my wide-eyed stories about Mt. SAC. I'd tell him about how once you run Mt. SAC you become part of a much larger cross-country brotherhood. The next year I took that emotion a step further. One of my girl runners won her race there. I pulled her aside and told her to remember that day. "You're part of an elite company now," I told her. "No matter where you go from here in life, no matter what you do, you won Mt. SAC. No one can ever take that away from you."

You've got to be a cross-country runner to fully appreciate that statement, but it's true. Winning Mt. SAC is one of the greatest achievements in running.

My best was a fourth. I can still remember the burning in my lungs as I attacked up the Switchbacks. It felt reckless and bold to make such a move when everyone else was dying. I paid the price, which is why I can also remember that weak-legged feeling of arriving atop Reservoir, not at all sure I had the strength to finish. Mt. SAC is a brutal course, demanding equal parts guts and speed. You don't so much race it as endure.

In my third year of coaching, Devin decided to condition for lacrosse by running cross-country. He did so grudgingly. One of my other sons, Connor, was beginning his freshman year and would also be running. As a dad, I was thrilled to be coaching my sons. But I was also apprehensive. See, my boys' teams had never been very good. I didn't want my sons to experience the humiliation of a losing season.

Some things can't be helped. At a vital league meet, the girls held their own against some very fierce competition, while the boys did so poorly that four of the last five finishers were from my squad. Devin's mood took a turn. We grew separate and angry with each other. He couldn't see his improvement as a runner. All he knew was that he'd heard sympathy applause on the final straight. "Pity applause" he called it. Having Connor get closer each and every race certainly didn't help.

The weeks went past. The annual countdown to Mt. SAC drew ever shorter. After all I'd told my sons about the course and all the times I'd glorified the act of suffering required to run it at your best, they were less than overjoyed when that hallowed day arrived. As the team walked the course, I tried to explain strategy but was met by hostile stares from the boys' team. They were edgy and afraid. Nobody wanted a repeat of the pity applause.

Connor's freshman race went off early in the afternoon, and he surprised himself with a breakout performance and a top-ten finish. He came to me, sweaty and proud, his medal hanging around his neck. Connor threw his arms around me, and I didn't mind a bit when my shirt became soaked in his sweat. That look of relief and glory on his face was priceless.

Devin and the varsity boys looked on, trying to be happy for the freshmen. But they were a sullen lot. Their race was still two long hours away, and they weren't so much dreading it as they were looking forward to getting it over with. I quietly felt the same. I was tired of the hostility and wariness, and I feared what would happen if they failed once again.

Mt. SAC is a spectator course, but you've got to be ready to run if you want to catch the action. I was at the end of the Runway when the race began, watching the boys' field charge toward me. "Be aggressive," I yelled, knowing by a flick of their eyes that they'd heard. "Stay smooth," I yelled as they began that second flat loop. Then I charged halfway up Switchbacks to wait for them. "Time to go to work," I yelled as they passed, a reminder that our prerace strategy revolved around a solid first mile and a powerhouse ascent.

My guys were bunched together midpack. Devin soon attacked, bringing two other runners with him. I watched as they moved up, and then I cut across the course to Poop-Out.

The strain was showing when my guys finally passed by three minutes later. Their faces were tired and lined. Their legs were heavy. They willed themselves forward, resisting the urge to chop their stride and ease their suffering.

And then I was sprinting again, taking the shortcut up Reservoir. It was the last time I would be able to cheer for them. They arrived at the top tightly bunched. "Less than three minutes left, Dev," I yelled. On this day, he stepped up when the team's top runner had a mental meltdown, and now Dev was my team's leader. The others were right behind. They charged after him, and I watched from on high as they sprinted down the backside of Reservoir, then kicked that long, flat quarter-mile known as the Gauntlet into the finish.

It was done, and without a whit of pity applause. I jogged back down the hill. I wouldn't get a chance to debrief the boys until later, because it was time for the girls to run. Soon I was in the midst of their race, doing all that crazy running once again, yelling the same crazy things.

Which is how I found myself atop Reservoir, returning Devin's call. "Dad," he said in a bubbly, childlike voice. I hadn't heard him sound like that since he was a Little Leaguer.

"Hey, sorry I hung up. I was—"

"Dad. We won. The boys won."

As a parent, you long for your children to know reward. You see their hard work and struggle, and you just pray that once in a while they get their moment in the sun.

Life doesn't always grant that wish. Every now and then, however, it does. When that moment comes, a deep wave of joy and thanks washes over you. And the greatest thing of all is that it's not about you. It's about your child, for whom you only want the best.

You remember that moment, and others like it, forever. You remember the courage on a young man's face as he pushes through yet another pain threshold in the third mile of a race that he dreaded. You remember a happy and unexpected phone call. You remember standing on a patch of dead grass atop a legendary hill, punching the air like a giddy fool.

And you remember putting on sunglasses so no one can see you cry.

THE BEER TRUCK

I came upon the beer truck while walking out of Starbucks last October. It was not just any beer truck but a refrigerated keg-and-bottle hauler belonging to the incomparable Stone Brewery out of nearby Escondido. They are, perhaps, the *Keep pushing . . . always* of microbreweries, with beers of defiant character and bold taste. "You are not worthy," reads the inscription on their Arrogant Bastard Ale. A lengthy fine-print treatise on the back of the amber bottle reminds anyone whose taste errs toward light yellow beers that this ale will be too much for them. That they will not enjoy it, so just don't bother trying in the first place.

I am, as it happens, a fan. Stone beers are like a fine Zinfandel or a well-marbled New York strip, a full-bodied experience to savor slowly and in moderation. One is more than enough—though I personally don't see any harm in having a second. And maybe, when the moon is full, a third.

Stone is a small brewery. Their delivery vehicles are not as common or noticeable as, say, a Pepsi truck. I'd never seen one before. In my mind, if I'd given the matter any thought at all, no such trucks existed. Stone beer was magically delivered to local super-markets in the dead of night, the way the tooth fairy appears and then vanishes.

So I was amused by this random sighting. It just so happened that the driver had parked next to my Suburban. He was stepping out to make a delivery. "You guys do a great job," I told him, just making conversation. Everyone likes a well-earned compliment.

The guy had a prominent earring, a graying soul patch, and a ponytail. His eyes got a paternal look, like those of an old wizened therapist. Stone is something of a cult. I can only imagine he is greeted by that sort of comment on a regular basis. "Yeah?" he asked. "Which one's your favorite?"

Where to begin? Stone comes out with a different version of their ales and stouts every couple of months. "I liked the thirteenth anniversary edition."

I must have had a faraway look in my eyes. He nodded indulgently and waited to see if I'd come up with any others.

"Oh, that's a favorite," he prompted in a kindly manner. Nice man.

"And the Russian stout."

He nodded. His eyes twinkled. "That's a good one, too."

Now, there's a pecking order with beverages. If I were talking to a wine delivery guy, the conversation might have a slightly elitist jargon. We'd talk about varietals and bouquet and vintages, and in some small way I'd be showing that I belonged to a segment of society that took the time to learn about the time-honored tradition of oenology. But beer appreciation is a bit rougher around the edges. Standing outside Starbucks and talking hops and barley was something of a phenomenon. Sort of a cross between discussing miter saws and mountain bikes—nothing too fancy, but with a specificity that keeps the conversation above the mundane. Still, is this sort of thing really done?

We said our good-byes. I was on my way. As chance would have it, I was off that day to Mt. SAC, where my team was racing in the invitational. It turned out to be a banner day. We won all sorts of races and medals.

The following week, on my way to a large and important meet that determined our postseason status, I happened to spy the Stone beer truck again right after I left my house. He was going one way, I was going the other. But two Stone sightings in as many weeks, after a lifetime of not seeing a single truck—could it be an omen?

I tucked that nugget away in the back of my head. But sure enough, another great day of racing. I am not superstitious, but all of a sudden I began wondering if there wasn't some sort of convergence. Maybe that Stone attitude about pushing limits with their beer was a subtle cosmic reminder to push myself as a coach on race day. It sounds insane, but remember that baseball players don't wash their socks when they're on a winning streak, and hockey players don't shave at all during the postseason. Could the Stone truck be my version of a play-off beard?

Another big race the next week. I left my home, intentionally pushing the Stone connection from my brain. But no sooner had I gone a mile than I saw the truck. Like I said, if we were talking Pepsi trucks or Domino's delivery cars or any other sort of garden-variety delivery vehicle, it would have been no big deal. But I'm sure that if I called the Stone Brewery to inquire about the number of trucks they sent out each day, we wouldn't be talking more than a dozen.

This was getting weird. Again, my team ran lights-out.

The obviously strange aspect of all this is that I was beginning to believe that a beer delivery truck was a message from God, sent to divine the fates of a group of young runners far too young to drink. I certainly didn't tell them about these mysterious sightings or invoke Stone in some prerace pep talk. And it's not like each success was somehow toasted by Stone products. Not at all. The connection existed in a bubble all its own. I didn't ask any questions. I didn't fall on my knees and pray for a truck sighting before the next race. I just reminded myself that omens come in all shapes and sizes. Why should a beer truck be excluded from the list?

The next week was the regional championships. Yes, I saw the truck. And yes, my team ran better than ever before. It was on to the state meet.

Which presented a dilemma: We were leaving Southern California, driving six hours north to Fresno for our race. But I could only assume that Stone might be sold somewhere up there. Not that I was calling Stone to check or Googling their Web site to find locations. Honest. But I kept my own counsel, figuring that if our good omen was going to show itself, it would be a true sign instead of a marvelous coincidence.

We boarded the bus and drove to Fresno. Not a Stone truck in sight. We jogged the course the day before the race, and still no sign of that truck. Back at the hotel, I took the team out to dinner. We walked. I kept a sharp eye out for that truck, just in case.

It was not to be. I'm a believer in dreams. I'm a believer that sometimes God speaks to us directly, in strange and miraculous ways. I'm a believer that there are such things as omens, or at least foreshadowing, if our eyes are open enough to look for it. But I don't believe in luck. Which, as Branch Rickey once noted, is "the residue of design."

For six long months I'd planned our season. Each workout, each interval, each mile pace. I read books, I spoke with the smartest running minds I could find, and I implemented this new knowledge in the training. I demanded absurd performance from my athletes, on absurd terrain and under sometimes absurd conditions. My runners made their own luck through hard work, perseverance, and a growing belief that if they pushed their personal limits each and every day, they could not fail.

And they didn't. That final meet was a smashing success. We finished second in the entire state of California.

Life is like that. Hard work and a well-followed plan produce spectacular results. There is no shortcut to success, except that which comes through striving every day to be our best. We look for a sign that things are going to be all right—some glance or nod that tells us we're on the right path, even when we already know it. Random reassurance is a powerful thing. Some days I see it in an e-mail or a well-written sentence or just that old friend who calls to pick me up when I have become unexpectedly blue. Those tokens become armor that we strap on to feel protected when life has us feeling most vulnerable.

I haven't seen a Stone truck since. I like to think that the Almighty enjoyed a small chuckle over my sightings. I have a sign on my office wall that reads: "Good morning. This is God. I will be handling all your problems today. I will not need your help. So have a nice day." Who's to say that truck wasn't a neat little cosmic joke to distract me from the nerves that so often have me bouncing off walls on race days?

Or maybe just a truck.

HARD-EARNED
WISDOM

DEEP THOUGHTS

The other morning, while engaged in that esteemed writerly tradition known as procrastinating, I came across a short psychological treatise on the Internet. The author was attempting to explain how we think when we run. "Associative" thoughts mean paying attention to our bodies, while "dissociative" is a preference for distraction. Whether running or not, I tend to wander back and forth through those twilight zones, paying close attention at times and zoning out at others. It is an odd trait of mine that the things I find most uncomfortable are the things that grab me by the face mask, so to speak. Yet I float through the enjoyable stuff, sometimes barely remembering it at all.

I never know whether I am associating or dissociating. It just happens. I can walk out of a three-hour Springsteen concert, head buzzing with euphoria, and not pinpoint a defining moment, even though I could have sworn I was fully absorbed the whole time.

With running, I connect associative and dissociative with specific performance expectations. The other day, for instance, I dropped down onto a trail that had recently been battered by rains of biblical proportions. It was the Live Oak Trail, a path I have run more than any other. I know each twist and turn by heart. But the storms had broken off tree branches, toppled mighty oaks, and forced a nearby stream to overflow. Its waters had cut great gashes in the trail and scrubbed away the topsoil. The hundreds of Chihuahua-size rocks once hidden beneath the surface now littered the ground like so many ankle-breaking obstacles.

I noticed all of these things in vivid detail during the first two miles of our run. The pace was light, and the physical act of running was incidental. My ears and eyes and ankles were the focus. This is what it means to dissociate. Or, as I like to think of it: enjoying the scenery.

After those first two miles, I raced some mountain bikers up a switchback. It took everything I had to keep up. I was cognizant of each footfall, my arm angles, my breathing patterns. I'd like to say there was someone slow enough to be running behind me, but that would be a lie. I knew that, too.

I knew the pine-scented loop I'd be running but had forgotten how impossibly far it was to the turnaround point. What had seemed like a short trot on an easy (dissociative) day was actually more than a thousand meters. The grade, which had seemed so flat when I envisioned it in my mind, was actually slightly uphill on the outbound portion and wonderfully downhill after we rounded the cinder block public restroom and pushed back to the start, poised to do it all again. I paid attention. I was in the moment. Time slowed down, expanding itself into the minutiae of running. The two-minute rest periods, on the other hand, flew past in what felt like five seconds.

This is associative running.

Racing feels like this, too, but with a profoundly higher level of focus and clarity. Call it associative squared. I know that some people like to dissociate during racing, to take their mind off the pain. But I'm so easily distracted that a moment's dissociation takes me to some distant emotional place from which I cannot return. The race seems suddenly unimportant. At the Raid Gauloises in Ecuador a few years back, I dissociated while walking across an Andean plain on the fourth day. Within minutes, I was thinking of all the better ways I could be using my personal time. Out of nowhere I decided to quit the race.

This is dangerous territory. The Navy SEALs point out that once someone has made the decision to quit basic training, there's no turning back. The mind has faltered long before the physical act of ringing the bell has taken place. What saved me in Ecuador was sharing this impulsive decision with a teammate. She reminded me that I was in no way fatigued or injured, merely bored by the scenery. Armed with this revelation, I carried on.

Okay. So we have associative and dissociative. But I would posit that there is another mental state comprising a little of both. It's the hyperfocus before the run, which then carries over into the workout so that it passes in such a blur that it's as if it never happened. Case in point: any day that my writing is going well. It's my habit on these days to get our boys off to school, write for a couple of hours to get the synapses firing, then go for a run to let all those new ideas percolate. Afterward, I'll head back into the office and write for three or four more hours, weaving together all those

endorphin-laced, highly oxygenated thoughts. My best writing—
or, I should say, my most fulfilling writing—has emanated from
this process. I've got the basic idea, I add a little run, then I plunge
back into the written word. No phone calls, no e-mails, no distrac-
tions. An introvert's dream.

Sometimes, however, I plunge too deep into the psyche.
These are my bunker days. I am so consumed by writing that I
am transported to another time and place. I do not exist, other
than as a vessel for whatever thought needs to flow onto the page.
Only reluctantly and perhaps out of obligation will I break away
for a run.

These are scary times. I am physically running, but my brain
is still writing. These are the runs where I stand at a stoplight and
run a hand across the drape of my running shorts, just to make
sure I remembered to get properly dressed. My fear is that one day I
will be standing on a street corner, naked and oblivious, trying to
figure out a story point even as the officers come to take me away.
These are the runs where I look back and forth two or three times
before crossing the street. In my mental condition, I might actually
forget why I'm looking both ways and sprint out in front of a car. A
run like this can last an hour. All the while I am associating in a
monster way with writing, while apparently dissociating from my run.

Here's the weird part: The spell is broken if I run to the top of
a hill. The whole way up will be a grind that will not register in the
slightest, but once I stand atop Chiquita Ridge or the hill I like to call
Falcon, or that spot on the Live Oak Trail where I have a
360-degree view of my world, I snap from my reveries. Very often

I will pause to appreciate what I'm seeing. Sometimes I offer a short prayer of thanks for the tremendous beauty or for the sudden lightness of my being. Summits purify me. They let me see. It's no wonder that on the morning of my wedding, I went for a run and somehow found myself listening to the wind atop a treeless, dun-colored hill that smelled of dry grass and dew. It just happens.

I don't know the clinical term for this hyperfocus and then the loosening of one's cares that occurs when all of the world is laid before me in some glaring display of perspective and beauty. I don't want to know.

Someone shared a quote with me a few years back, something to the effect of "To judge a man's intellect, test the firmness of his thigh." Obvious ramifications about pushing your thumb into strange men's thighs aside, I understand the sentiment. To run is to think. To think is to solve problems, dream, reflect, hope, mourn, pray, and grow. We focus so much on the way running tones our thighs and fortifies our hearts, but running is also a spiritual and emotional journey.

The world is a busy place, and busyness is not conducive to random thoughts. Stepping out the door for a run is like recess for the psyche. Whether associating or dissociating, we come back refreshed—or, at the very least, whole.

BRUISED AND BATTERED

"Is that the spot?"

The needle poked into my heel from the outer edge, existing in that paper-thin universe between the bottom of my calcaneus and the sole of my right foot. "Yes," I said after a second's hesitation.

"No, no, no. You'll be sure when you feel it." The doctor pressed the needle in further. I lay facedown on the table, unable to see the long hypodermic. All I knew was that it hurt. Like hell. I don't mean that as a figure of speech, but that's exactly how it felt—as if my heel had been lowered into the fiery depths.

Then, of course, my foot burst into flames.

My leg clenched like a fist. Wildfire raced from the very bottom of my foot all the way up my spine and into my brain, making me grit my teeth and inhale sharply. It wasn't the most painful thing I'd ever felt in my life—that would have been the day Patricia Lee kicked me in the genitals with her black patent leather shoes when I was ten. (All my fault, incidentally. She had threatened to kick me there. I'd never been kicked there before. So I stood tall and said, "Go ahead.") But this was definitely the sharpest and most specific.

"Ah, that's the spot." The doctor chuckled at my misery, though more likely it was the satisfaction of getting it right. "Okay, hold still." It turns out we were just getting started. Finding the bruise on my heel's fat pad was a prelude to the injection of the molten lava known as cortisone that would make my heel feel all better.

A cortisone shot is not, sadly, a brisk process. The physician doesn't just jam down on the plunger that forces medicine out the tip of the needle. No, the doctor applies the easiest and slowest pressure possible, allowing the precious cortisone to seep into the painful area just like that lazy, unstoppable flow of lava slowly consuming portions of Hawaii's Big Island, washing over cars and stop signs and homes until all that exists is a thick black coating. Beneath that thick crust, everything is dead.

In my case, the deadness referred to my swelling and pain. Within moments of the injection, my heel was magically healed.

How did I get to this point? First off, I leapt from a steeple-chase barrier midrace and landed wrong. I didn't notice anything at the time, but during a long run the next day, I began hobbling for no reason. This led to several attempts at convincing myself that the pain would go away overnight or with ice or heat or ibuprofen—none of which helped. This led to a week off from training, which meant a week of rehabbing by swimming in a pool and riding a stationary bike, both of which I consider cruel and inhuman forms of boredom. When things didn't get better after a week, I laced up my shoes and bolted out for a run, only to pull up lame and near tears from the amazing pain within three steps.

Another week on the bike and in the pool. Another week after that. At one point the school's athletic trainer crafted an ingenious pad for my heel that looked very much like a miniature version of those inflatable pillows favored by hemorrhoid patients. He spent a great deal of time finding the right cushioning and snipping away at it with surgical scissors before slipping it into my shoe. That didn't work, either.

Then, just when I was beginning to ponder a life without running, I heard about The Shot. The rest was history.

That's the way it is with running injuries. They creep into your life like a thief in the night and steal the keys to that car known as your body. No matter how many times you study the problem, looking for a solution, you find yourself unable to take that car out for a spin.

I'm not a patient person. Inactivity makes me hostile. Running has the exact opposite effect. So when I can't run at all, I go through the Kubler-Ross grief cycle. When I come to the part about acceptance, I relax a little and remind myself to settle in and make the best of things. The fact of the matter is that injuries need time to go away. Rushing them invariably leads to relapse, which leads to more frustrating weeks off. I'm not saying that I have acquired some sort of magical patience that now allows me to immediately accept my injury and suspend all activity until it is gone. No, I still grit my way through a run or two, hobbling like a complete moron who lacks the common sense to know better. But I'm getting better at it.

It's a lesson I have learned to apply to my runners. I hate when they get injured. I examine their precious conditioning level, the one that has taken weeks and months of carefully planned training, and despair that it will wither as they rehab. Last year I was quite proud that my team had gone injury free for almost the whole season, when suddenly a half dozen runners were struck down by shin-splints and patellar tendinitis and even a stress fracture. I got mad at first—not at them but at the random nature of injury, which can feel so cruel. The short list of sudden ways to get sidelined is not that short—and includes plantar fasciitis (the tendon sheaths on the foot tightening into quivers of pain), pulled muscles (groin, psoas, soleus, hamstring, glute, quad, and even lower back), those annoying shin splints, the agony of patellar tendinitis, and the injury whose name we dare not speak: the dreaded torn Achilles tendon.

Seen in that light, it's no wonder that my runners get injured. It's a wonder that they don't get injured more. I have come to believe that the body is a marvelous machine, resilient and strong. Injury is that grain of sand in the oyster shell, the irritant that shows us where our body is weak, reminding us not to just heal but to find a way to make that part stronger.

Not being able to run is not the same as being inactive. Sometimes that time away prevents staleness and overuse. Sometimes an injury is just what the doctor ordered.

With my runners, I practice prevention. Weights and hills and plyometrics build peripheral systems like ligaments and tendons and smaller muscle groups that tend to be overlooked. We ice bath after almost every practice. I emphasize hydration, sleep, and proper eating. I pay close attention to their running shoes, looking for compressed midsoles and other signs of wear. And I pray, because at some point it's out of my hands. Bodies break down. It's a fact of life.

When an injury occurs, I do the only thing possible and get them on the bike and in the pool and even onto Satan's boring handmaiden, the elliptical exercise machine. Most of all, I just wait. Their bodies will be ready when they are ready. I would never suggest cortisone for any of them, even if it would hasten the process. It seems wrong to put such a powerful solution in bodies that are still growing and transforming. I wonder if that stuff actually inhibits healing in some way by making it easier to run before the body is better.

But it works for me, and I've had two more cortisone injections in the bottom of my foot to combat plantar fasciitis. The injections were always my last resort when an injury just wouldn't go away. The part of me that remembers the injection scene from *North Dallas Forty* all too well, however, has nagged at me every time I've gotten the shot. Might I be inadvertently breaking my body down just for the sake of a few less weeks of rehab?

I was working out in the House of Pain a while back when someone shot a lacrosse ball out of a cannon straight into my calf. After I'd collapsed to the ground, infuriated that someone could do such an evil thing, I looked over to where I thought the ball might have landed, so I could throw it back at the perpetrator.

But there was no lacrosse ball. And the only other people in the gym were Sedge and Crash, who are not the sort to engage in midsession frivolity. I'd torn a muscle in my leg from doing explosive leaping exercises.

There was no way I could have even pretended to run, so I girded myself for the mandatory time off that was sure to come. I was introduced to the world of modern sports medicine in the form of a facility that helps Olympic and professional athletes heal more quickly. After two weeks of being unable to walk any faster than a slow limp, I was fully recovered after just one therapy session. Heat, electric stim, and some sort of voodoo did the trick.

And while I was oh so glad to be running again, part of me somewhat perversely missed the downtime that comes with a longer healing process. I must have needed a break. So, strange as it seems, I give thanks for my injuries. They keep me mentally fresh, they allow my body a chance to build itself up when it is weak, and they make me appreciate the gift of running more than I can ever say.

PROCESS
(THE LITTLE THINGS)

"The process is the goal."

That's a saying you hear a lot from distance coaches. It's not much different from "work the process" or just "process" as a verb. It applies to almost any journey from point A to point B, although the most gratifying come with adventures, setbacks, comebacks, hard-won kernels of self-knowledge, and sometimes even a championship.

From a coaching perspective, working the process is the daily act of ensuring that runners do activation drills, race-appropriate workouts, hydration, sleep, mobility, hex-bar dead lifts, hill repeats, neuromuscular strides, and the hundreds of other little things that comprise a successful training evolution.

Anyone can do the big things, but only champions do the little things, goes another saying.

This is the coach in me talking, but I find that people without a process lose their way. They invariably value outcome above all else, not wanting to endure the suffering, despair, and innovation that constitutes a journey. Thus, they rarely see the outcome they desire.

I think of all this because I was listening to a favorite podcast the other day. I've become quite the fan of podcasts. I never listen to music when I run, but I often pass time on the spin bike or a long car ride listening to smart people riff on what works for them. Invariably, podcasts are about purpose. Which is good, because I'm always trying to find a way to do things just a little better, or to gain insight into the ways others attack a problem to see if I might glean a nugget of wisdom I can incorporate into my own journey.

Rare is the individual who trumpets their process as the best. That's the unwritten rule of podcasts. But while I was listening to a noted writer speak about his process, he made a comment that stung. After getting through the artsy stuff about finding oneself, and mantra, and the muse, and all the artifice that, frankly, gets in the way of putting words on the page, this guy spoke disparagingly about writers who practice a daily regimen. He suggested that those who made writing a discipline were mostly "old white guys whose wife brings them lunch every day."

That's an actual quote.

The best way to be truly creative, this writer suggested, is to go alone to a hotel room or a writer's retreat or a mountain cabin. Turn off your phone, call room service, and vomit words onto the page. Write all night and sleep all day. When you've finished the project, stop writing until it's time to start a new one. This, the author suggested, is the one true process.

I think that's bullshit.

I also think this individual wishes someone would bring him lunch every day.

I'm not old, at least in my own head. But I'm white. My muse is my mortgage. I think of myself as creative, though there are times when I can't put two sentences together. Most of all, I write each and every day.

Love it. Adore it. Rise at dawn. Pot of coffee. *LA Times* front page to back. Then, although I am well aware that sitting is the new smoking, I plop into my desk chair, fire up my laptop, and spend the next six hours fussing and fiddling with the English language. I write a thousand words some days, several thousand when I'm really rolling, and less than a hundred on others. I get cranky and even angry on days I don't write, just the same as I do on days when I don't run. So I do it. It's not a punctuation mark, like sex. It's a necessity, like breathing.

I've written in airports, cabins, tropical islands, movie sets, five-star hotel rooms, coffee shops, and just about anyplace in the world you can tap a keystroke. I once wrote two entire books while on location in the jungles of Borneo filming a season of *Survivor*. It's amazing how much you can accomplish if you spend fourteen hours a day in front of your laptop. The best is when I can write in my office—bookshelves, comfortable chair, a big wooden glorious mess of a desk.

That's my process, no more compulsive, obsessive, or restricted to white guys than brushing my teeth.

Running is like that. There's no single way to run. Those "little things" I mentioned aren't a one-size-fits-all checklist—they're a batch of good habits, yours to pick and choose as you like. When I'm working the process as a coach, my athletes get better. Not in the course of a single workout, but over time. When the process is over, if all goes well, we've had twenty-two weeks of pushing limits and human connection resulting in amazing performance improvement. These are memories my runners will carry forever.

It was once explained to me that neuromuscular connections are like a grassy pasture. If you walk through that field from time to time, you'll press down on the grass, leaving behind a slight impression that quickly springs back. But if you walk through that field every day, following the same route each time, that grass will give way to a path, then a clearly defined trail. Over time, it will become a highway.

The pathway from mind to muscles becomes a superhighway if we repeat an action again and again. When we stop, or take a long break, the path grows over. Working the process means walking the path every day, or at least on a regular basis, having a specific plan of who you are, where you're going, and why you're headed in that direction. The gait becomes surer, running economy is more athletic (hips forward, shoulders back, eyes up, each footfall landing directly beneath the center of gravity), and muscles don't rebel at the act of running—a feat we are biomechanically engineered to accomplish with relative ease. When you take a break, you will have to start the painful process of tamping down that trail all over again.

There I go, defining the process, just like that writer on the podcast. That's wrong of me. So find your own way. Write your own rules. Adopt the little things in your own life that make you better, defining the process in your own unique way—then work it.

Bon voyage.

TIME AND AGAIN

If I had my way, runners the world over would be banned from jogging in place at stoplights. Immediately. I would also like to see an international ban on the clicking of the sports watch to the "pause" setting at stoplights, for reasons I am about to explain.

First, let's address the "jogging in place" thing: You know who you are. Stop doing it. Just stop. It accomplishes nothing and, quite frankly, looks silly.

Now that we've got that out of the way, let's focus on the stopping of stopping time. The rationale for the click is that stoplight time prevents a runner from getting an accurate record of the precise number of minutes that were run by the end of the workout, as well as the precise pace per mile.

The last thing I do before slipping out for a run is check the time. I don't wear a watch, but I like to know how long I'll be out. If I'm parked at a trailhead, that means taking one last peek at my phone or turning on the battery power in my car so that the digital display flicks on. At home it means looking at the cable box. Sometimes I forget, but most days I don't. A long time ago I learned that running for time beats running for distance any day of the week. My training week is comprised of hours, not miles. An average week is five. Anything less is not so good. Nine or ten means I'm getting serious about some coming race, or maybe I just need some alone time in the hills.

But my five hours might easily be five hours and seven minutes. Or four hours and forty-nine minutes. Or even five hours and thirty-five minutes. The difference might be the length of time I might have to wait for a signal down at the busy Alicia–Santa Margarita Parkway crossroads. I like to walk a little after I finish my run, so I'll stroll all sweaty and tired for five minutes or so. Maybe more, maybe less. If I'm feeling contemplative, I'll sit on my porch and take off my shoes, then sit barefoot by the lavender bush and appreciate the calm that comes with a good day on the trail. Maybe I'll sip a bottle of water—or not, if I'm in the mood to step on the scale. I like to cheat the weight gods by weighing myself only after a very long day when I sweat every last bit of carbohydrate- and sodium-induced water gain from my cells. It's an illusion, I know. But it makes me feel good about myself.

I digress. Anyway, sometimes I do all those things before checking the postrun time. This forces me to estimate how many minutes have passed since I got done running. So while seventy minutes have passed since I started out, maybe it's been about twelve since I finished. I call it fifteen, just so I'm not slacking too much. Doing this day after day is how I assemble my hours per week of running.

Those of you who compulsively click your watches at stoplights, train crossings, bathroom breaks, Central Park horse carriages, and any of a million other little nuisances that can bring your run to a halt are by now rolling your eyes. You are referencing your running logs, with their to-the-second indications of training time. You have recorded your morning pulse rate. You have recorded your morning weight, which, as we all know, fluctuates wildly, based on the size of last night's steak and whether or not you actually enjoyed the meal with niceties like mashed potatoes or spinach or a green salad or you simply trimmed off all the fat, ate exactly half of the steak, then washed it all down with a big glass of water instead of the hearty Zinfandel it truly deserves. And most of all, you are aghast at the mere suggestion that a day's run should not be quantified, scrutinized, and recorded for posterity. Whose posterity, I don't know. I can't remember the last time someone shuffled off this mortal coil and his descendants relived the good old days by poring over the dead man's training logs.

I kept a log once. Years ago. It was one of those red Jim Fixx training books. I will admit that it kept me honest. I could look at it and say that I ran six days this week, five this one, and seven the week after that, which undoubtedly made that week the most successful of all. I knew my daily, weekly, and monthly mileage. I knew pace per mile. I knew which courses I'd run. All of that. Since this sort of accountability is supposed to go hand-in-glove with maturity or responsibility or whatever barometer one chooses to judge the alleged quality of a man's life, I felt slightly guilty when I

stopped keeping that log. So much so that, as late as last summer, I
kept a log on flotrackr.org—for all of three weeks.

The reason I stopped is the same reason I stopped inking miles
in the Fixx log—it took the fun out of running. Running is not
always a carefree pastime. It's hard work some days, with little or
no joy to show for the effort. But even on those days when the trail
is lined by rattlers, the Santa Ana winds are drying my lips and
that skin between my thighs that is so fond of chapping, and all
those wonderful equestrian fanatics are clogging the trail with their
weekend horseback outings (plus deposits), it's still a good day. It's
still the thing I'd rather be doing than almost anything else. The
day I stopped worrying about miles run, pace, time to the second,
and all that other stuff that clogs the brain was the day I learned
how running can make you feel in the moment. Present. The day is
long gone when I'm going to win the car at my local road race, so
why does it matter how long I am running? My wife often com-
plains, and rightfully so, that I am a pain to run with because my
curiosity overwhelms me. I see a new trail and I need to explore.
I find myself at a fork where I'd planned to turn left, but instead I
go right. I don't know why. I just do. Some days I go longer than I
should. Some days I go shorter.

But throughout, the run is the thing. Back when I kept obsessing about the length of my workouts, it was all about the logbook—
the tail wagging the dog. It made no sense to explore or to take that
unplanned right turn. That would have fouled up the exact length
of my course, which would have fouled up my split for the day,
which means it would have compared unfavorably with a similar

split from a week earlier. And then, see, I would have moped. I would have spent the rest of the day wondering why I'd run slower. (Or worse, on a day when I'd run faster, the initial euphoria would fade away and I'd begin to fear I might never be capable of going that fast again.)

The Kenyans like to let their bodies dictate training pace. They tend to run in groups, and on days when the legs don't feel the calling, they drop down to a slower group. When the legs have it going on, they're up there with the lead pack.

Which brings me to the hypocrisy of my timeless running philosophy. It's okay for me to run without a watch, not keep a log, and pause midrun to gape at the Pacific. And I do the same for the runners I coach, sending them off on runs that exist solely for recovery, strength, or sightseeing.

But when they're on the track, I'm all about the watch. I don't own a single running watch, but I own a dozen stopwatches. I log their workouts. On a spreadsheet. Which I open frequently and gaze upon, thinking deep thoughts about what worked and what didn't. I am, as a coach, everything I am not as a runner. I have to be. Elite athletes need to know detail, structure, and an awareness that their coach is obsessing about all those things so they don't have to. They have a balance in their schedule between striving to tame the clock and those days where we go for what's called an adventure run and forget about time altogether.

Elite running is but a small fraction of a runner's life. Five years for some. Ten to twenty for the very lucky. Someday my runners will no longer be elite. It's my hope that as they mature into complex adults, they continue running. I think this means, as it should for all of us, that once you leave the elite realm, the daily obsession with the watch, logbooks, and detail-oriented running should be replaced by a true love of being in the moment, enjoying all the charms running provides.

One of the great downfalls of the modern running movement is how anal and joyless some of its leading voices have made it. Think of me as that great voice in the wilderness that says it's okay to have fun out there.

Throw the logbook away. Stop pausing your watch at stoplights. Go right when you meant to go left.

Wander.

THE "C" WORD

My wife and I flew up to Ferndale for a wedding last summer. It's a farm town with a Victorian main street up near the Oregon border. The ceremony wasn't until 6:00 p.m., so we had a day to fill. After breakfast on the main drag, we wandered past the volunteer fire station and into a bookstore, where we asked for directions to the county fair. This seemed like a brilliant way of killing several hours, which is how we soon found ourselves in an enormous barn rife with the smell of livestock and alfalfa, watching goats with enormously swollen udders being paraded before a young female judge wearing thick glasses and a pantsuit. She appraised each of the animals in a knowing way before handing out blue ribbons to the winners.

I had never given goats much thought, but I found myself wondering if maybe raising a few competitive goats would be a nice pastime. They looked cute enough, and it seemed like there wouldn't be much to it. They could live in the backyard. Not that we have that sort of room, but Callie and I could make it work.

But as with all new endeavors, you don't know what you don't

know. What seemed simple on the surface would become an obsession. I like to win. I'm not embarrassed to say it. And all-consuming
passion is very often what it takes to win.

Soon enough I'd be visiting goat websites, laughing at insider
jokes about goat life, visiting a top breeder in some faraway town to
purchase an extremely expensive prospective champion show goat,
and basically filling my life with goats, goats, goats. It wouldn't be
enough just to win a small-town fair. I'd be jetting all over the
country with my goats, eventually hoping to show my expertise by
winning a national championship. If there is such a thing as goat
Olympics, chances are I'd be trying to win that, too.

It would funny if it wasn't true. I've followed that competitive
rabbit hole all my life, first with running, then writing, and most
lately with coaching. The initial desire to just go out there and have
fun becomes a burning desire to be the very best.

It will take over your life if you let it.

Which is why it bothers me when people claim they don't care
about winning and losing. Runners are the worst of these liars. "I
am *not* competitive," some insist. These people say it, spitting with
disdain, as if it's the other "c" word.

But every runner competes. You see it most easily among the
elite. Less obvious is the back of the pack, such as those who stop at
a pre-arranged spot a half-mile from the finish, where a waiting
loved one hands them their finisher's medals from previous races,
to be proudly (and loudly, given the heavy weight and metallic con-
struction of medals nowadays) worn before the crowds lining the
finish chute.

You see it in the costume runners trying to outdo one another for most outlandish attire or shiniest sequins on their running skirt, or garnering astonished looks from the crowd as they scuttle past in full Mary Poppins regalia, right down to the handbag, umbrella, and cute little hat pinned neatly in place. You overhear it in conversation at the coffee shop, as men and women who would otherwise consider themselves casual runners disclose their half-marathon times. The slower runner almost always emits a sheepish response, something like "I didn't really train for it."

It gets fun when the reply is a brutal, "Neither did I."

And then there's the third "c" word.

"She cheated," my wife informed me of someone she has known for years.

Calene swears she is not competitive.

"I was ten minutes ahead of her at the turnaround, then she magically crosses the finish line five minutes in front of me. But she never passed me. I'm sure she cut the course."

A week later, and Calene still wouldn't let it go. "She's a cheater," she reminded me when the woman's name came up over a glass of wine. We were sitting in the backyard, right about where the goats would be sleeping.

"Maybe you didn't see her go by," I replied. "Maybe she passed you at an aid station while you were drinking water."

I'm such a fool sometimes.

"She cheated. And now she's telling people that she beat me," said Callie, her tight-lipped scowl ending what until then had been a very promising romantic conversation. She took her wine glass and walked inside, though not before adding: "I don't know how she can live with herself."

It's not just running. A lady down the cul-de-sac used to brag when her kids pooped in a toilet for the first time, tied their shoes for the first time, and rode their bikes without training wheels for the first time. She was just being proud. But what I heard was that my own sons—none of whom seemed in any hurry to conquer any of those milestones—were destined for lives of menial labor and an addiction to daytime television.

I pretended not to care. "I'll start worrying if they aren't potty-trained by age thirty," I would joke.

But I seethed. It's been twenty-five years. I still haven't let it go.

There is part of me that wants to be at peace and ignore the competitive side of life. To not judge my visit to the bank by whether I choose the fastest line, and am thus somehow a winner. To not care when I get cut off in traffic. To hear footsteps approaching from behind during a trail run and just be content to let that person pass by, offering a chipper hello and a friendly comment on the sunshine as they trot past.

Impossible.

Last night I woke up at 3:00 a.m. My mind was filled with worry. I tried to pinpoint the source. That's always a good way to fall back to sleep: specify the anxiety, realize that in the light of day it will (most likely) be an insignificant blip, then console myself with that knowledge and return to a deep slumber.

Turns out I wasn't worrying. I was planning. My mind was constructing workouts and pace charts for my runners. With the first race of a new cross-country season just two weeks away, I was making myself miserable micromanaging Week Ten of a twenty-two week training cycle, terrified that I was missing some vital component of aerobic development.

Why? Because I want to win. And I know other coaches are doing the same. One of the most sublime sensations a runner can know is crossing the finish line first. For a cross-country team, it's standing as a group atop the podium, all those months of sweat and sacrifice ending the way they had long dreamed. I wouldn't be much of a coach if I didn't give my all to effect that outcome.

Life is competition. It just is. We're all the result of a zygote kicking ass on its way to the egg. That's where it starts, in literally our first moment of being.

So go out there and win something.

EPILOGUE:
TO BE A RUNNER

"Ever think of giving it a try?"

It had been a year since my knee surgery. Liam needed new running shoes, so we were back at our local shop, the same place where I decompensated after that morning at the symphony. My youngest son was now a senior captain on the JSerra cross-country team, tall, independent, and fully versed in the ritual of purchasing trainers and flats.

As Liam bounded off for a test jog, the salesman turned my way. He was new. Part of the myth about being a runner is that we all look alike. You hear people say it all the time: "He looks like a runner." It's code for lean, and sometimes a little too thin. But in truth, there's no singular shape for runners. The growth of running from a niche sport into the world's most popular form of exercise changed all that. Spectate for a morning at any 5-K or half-marathon and you'll see competitors of all girths and gaits. Each wears a race number and puts one foot in front of the other. Thus each and every one is a runner. Actually, they don't really need the race number—putting one foot in front of the other is proof enough.

Or, as I like to remind myself on those days when the pace lags and my legs feel like bricks, none of those people looking at me from their cars care about fast or slow. All they see is a runner.

I should not have been surprised when the running-store guy tried to double his sale. Yet I was devastated he didn't assume I was a runner. My identity has been tied up in running for as long as I can remember. The knee injury came out of nowhere, a sudden inflammation of the joint that occurred while training for Boston. I do not know precisely how I got hurt, because it basically went from a perfect knee to a swollen and incredibly painful gathering of ligaments, tendons, and cartilage. But a little online research showed me it was preventable: I sit too long during my writing day, don't stretch before running, increase my mileage before a marathon too quickly, don't drink enough water, and, like most runners, was surprised to find that I have very weak hip muscles.

One fact was certain: cartilage in the knee joint is supposed to slide against itself five times smoother than ice on ice. Decade after decade of taking my body for granted had my right knee grating like a bag of rocks.

The surgeon was a triathlete. There was every hope he would give me the green light to run as soon as the procedure was complete. Instead, in the spirit of preventative medicine, he suggested I train the same way he did—swimming, biking, and very little running.

But I didn't want to be a triathlete. I didn't want to be callous in my personal relationships, anal-retentive about my training logs, shave my legs, sport an m-dot tattoo, and endlessly obsess about the correlation between caloric intake and bowel-movement consistency.

I just wanted to be a runner.

My body feels different—I would even say better—for having run. Even on days when life is complete shit, there is a moment when the mind, body, trail, and sensation of getting stupendously lost in the act of running leads to a palpable feeling that all is right with the world. I'm not talking about the runner's high—I'm saying that I feel closer to God.

Or, as my friend Terry Sedgewick, major domo of the House of Pain, states simply: "Running has a different sweat."

I was on crutches for five weeks after the surgery. I had no choice but to swim and bike. The knee felt wobbly for six months after that. It might have been in my head, but there was no way I could run on it without risking more injury.

I stuck with the mountain bike and pool. To mix things up, I sometimes ran in a flotation belt, legs churning as if I were in full stride, head barely above the waterline, eyes focused on the sycamore trees surrounding our community pool, pretending I was somewhere on a trail.

But I wasn't. I was in the special lane roped off for lap swimmers, with sunbathers on the deck and children splashing in the water just on the other side of the buoys. My presence was annoying to the lap swimmers, who had to swim around me during their relentless back-and-forth above the black line. I was completely aware that I was an awkward sight—an obstruction, a nuisance, a man clearly out of place—but at least I was accomplishing something that made me feel, if ever so slightly, like a runner.

Eventually, I'd pull myself up onto the deck. Sometimes I'd jog a barefoot lap on the grass at the park next door, ignoring the soccer nets that had no business cluttering the green expanse in the middle of baseball season. Every step hurt. I didn't yet know the importance of words like "mobility" and the need to strengthen my hips to take undue pressure off the knee. All I knew was that my leg still didn't feel right. Months passed. The pool running, mountain biking, and jogging on the grass became infrequent.

Then one day, I woke up and realized I was no longer a runner.

Not by any stretch of the imagination. The part of me that ran the hills as if they were my own property was no more. The body at rest stays at rest. The body in motion stays in motion. I had been at rest too long. My legs had forgotten how to do more than hobble. Running was for people from another planet. More than anything else, I was afraid of making my knee worse, and perhaps having another surgery.

So it was that the third time I got fat was after knee surgery.

It's what happens when life and fear get in the way of being the best version of myself. It's also the slow progression from medium to large, skipping completely over husky en route to XL. Inevitably, the physical side effects of gaining weight—such as high blood pressure, decreased flexibility, and just a wee bit less manliness when I needed it most—made themselves known. It had been fifteen years since that initial visit to the House of Pain. But if anything, I had let myself fall into worse shape than when I first set foot inside those doors.

I missed the things runners say without knowing it. "That would be a pretty running trail," my wife remarked one day on a train. We were in Norway, along the fjords. A narrow goat path cut through a thick green pasture, weaving along the contour of a long body of water covered in mist. I knew just what she meant.

I longed for the things runners can do that normal people are never, ever allowed to do in public. For instance, a man or woman in a business suit cannot discreetly answer the call to nature by jumping behind a tree. Runners can. Most do.

Runners spit and blow snot rockets and fart mid-stride while running up a hill surrounded by their best friends. They talk about their sex lives and politics and thoughts on religion; their children, their fantasies, and their failures; their finances, their self-image, and the ten things in life they fear most. There are no boundaries.

A male runner can go bare-chested on a city street any time of year, no questions asked. A female runner can do the same in a jog bra. Not so for the normal populace.

Runners write grocery lists, arguments, briefs, poems; calculate split times, family budgets, travel expenses, and the precise number of days to taper before the next big race—all in their heads, without speaking or even moving their lips, as the miles pass. Some ideas disappear like smoke before the run is over. The good stuff percolates in the subconscious, seemingly lost forever before presenting itself once again as a problem solved.

A runner has a love-hate relationship with race-day nerves. I call it "waking up nervous." Races are a reckoning. Trying to be a better version of you. This is physically, mentally, and emotionally painful. Who wouldn't be nervous?

In our household, it was now my wife who was waking up nervous. Callie had become the runner in our family. The woman who didn't know a trail ten years ago was suddenly running half-marathons and putting together her own small running group.

Ironically, I was more fixated on running than ever before, thanks to my ongoing role as a high school distance coach. It's been my avocation for almost two decades. I spend hours each week not just planning workouts and studying methodologies of the great coaches like Vigil and Daniels, but also reading new literature about subjects such as the active role of the central nervous system in our training. Not a day goes by that I don't plan, strategize, and strive to learn more about the science and art of distance running. Afternoons coaching my runners and forming friendships within the coaching community are some of the greatest blessings I have ever known.

I don't know whether to call it the butterfly effect or a snowball rolling downhill, but the universe eventually made itself known. Somewhat randomly, a few friends celebrated my birthday on social media by posting old photographs. I was running in almost all of them. I wanted to be that guy again. So I ran a little. A jog on the Live Oak Trail where no one could see me. A walk-run through Hyde Park where there were so many people witnessing my efforts that I was actually anonymous. Everything hurt. It was horrible. I couldn't believe that a sport that had once been so carefree, and which had physically sustained me for so many years, felt so damned hard.

So I stopped.

Which only made things worse. One September morning, as my team was wrapping up the first workout of the day, I walked into the neighborhood 7-Eleven to buy them post-workout chocolate milk. I get the kind with added protein. It's the perfect recovery drink.

The owner is an old friend who has done well for himself—well enough that he hadn't worked a day in the store for years. I waved when I walked in. He gave me a curious smile.

I gathered up the chocolate milk from the refrigerated section. There were sixteen in all. I hugged them in my arms to hold them as I stepped to the counter. A line started forming behind me.

"I almost didn't recognize you, Coach," my friend growled loudly. He's a big man whose voice is booming in normal conversation. Now it seemed to roar from the hot dog grill by the cash register all the way back to the beer case, falling on every ear in between. "You're so big. I've never seen you that large. Wow. You're really huge. You used to be so skinny. Have you been lifting?"

In a moment like that, all you think of is the draft pints of craft beer, that heated blueberry muffin at Starbucks, the many-many-*many* hamburgers and spicy hot wings that comprised dinner on the drive home from practice, the pizzas that didn't stop with just two slices, the instant fortification of fast-food burritos with extra onions, and basically every calorie I'd stuffed into my face with the exception of salads.

And I realized I had a choice.

I could find a way to grow old with a healthy balance of diet and exercise, once again working hard to become the athlete and lover I wanted to see when I looked in the mirror, knowing I could be there for Calene in mind, body, and spirit for decades to come.

Or I could choose not to.

"A man without self-discipline is like a city whose walls are falling down," I read in Proverbs not long after.

And the die was cast.

Time to be a runner—again.

How do you start all over?

My comeback began with humility, and by pretending I'd never run a step in my life. I followed all the lessons I preach to the kids I coach when they show up for their very first practice: buy good shoes, run and walk at first, run on dirt and grass whenever possible, and, most of all, show up every day. Consistency is the key to success in all things.

I added new elements to my training, things like mobility, hip-strengthening exercises, and a greater emphasis on daily core conditioning. For the millionth time in my life, I reminded myself that being a runner does not mean I can eat and drink anything I want.

And I returned once more to the House of Pain. "Nice to see you, Coach," said Terry Sedgewick, looking no older than he had on my first visit so long ago. "Let's get to work."

It's a simple sport, this endeavor of putting one foot in front of the other. Yet it's so damned hard.

That's what makes it great.

I'm not all the way back yet. But I'm out there every day. You don't know how much you miss a discipline until you embrace it again. It's an abused word, discipline. Yet nothing great happens without it.

It's easy to let up, ease back, lower expectations. But "Keep Pushing . . . Always," means just that. Always.

That's how to be a runner.

ACKNOWLEDGMENTS

Thanks to all my runners. It's my prayer that running will be part of your life for many years to come.

To Eric Simonoff, for the years of career guidance and friendship.

To the Tough Guy Book Club.

To my Mom and Dad.

To Devin, Connor, and Liam, with all my love.

And to Calene. You are my sunshine.

ABOUT THE AUTHOR

Martin Dugard, a *New York Times* #1 bestselling author and lifelong runner, has written about running and endurance sports for more than thirty years. He is also the coauthor of the narrative nonfiction Killing series, works of history with eighteen million copies in print. In addition, he is the head cross-country coach at JSerra Catholic High School in San Juan Capistrano, California.